CONTENTS

Standard Occupational Classification Volume 3

B

Office of Population Censuses and Surveys

Standard Occupational Classification
Volume 3

Social Classifications
and Coding Methodology

LONDON : HMSO

© Crown copyright 1991
First published 1991

ISBN 0 11 691338 X

British Library Cataloguing in Publication Data
Standard occupational classification
Vol. 2, Social classifications and coding methodology

1. Introduction

The following sections should be read in conjunction with the Introduction to the *Standard Occupational Classification Volume 1*. A number of the themes introduced there are discussed and illustrated in more detail in the present volume.

This volume:

- reviews the needs that SOC was designed to meet (Section 2);

- reviews the principles and concepts underlying the design of SOC (Section 3);

- explains how the SOC structure was developed, taking account of predecessor classifications and of limitations in the raw data to which it must be applied (Section 4);

- explains how Social Class and Socio-economic Group classifications are derived from SOC, using additional information on status in employment and size of employing establishment (Section 6);

- gives an account of continuity and discontinuity in detail between predecessor classifications and SOC and the classifications rebased on it (Sections 5 and 6);

- discusses some issues which arise in applying the socio-economic classifications (Section 7);

- indicates the degree of compatibility between SOC and the 1988 version of the International Standard Classification of Occupations (Section 8); and

- describes arrangements for introducing SOC in central government applications (Section 9).

In the text a number of different classifications, statistical sources, and technical terms are introduced. To avoid cumbersome repetition abbreviations are often used. In case readers find these initially hard to recall and distinguish, a list with interpretations is provided as Appendix C. Figure 1 at Section 4.2 provides an overview of the SOC classificatory structure. Figure 2, also at Section 4.2, shows in summary diagrammatic form the interrelationships between the various classifications discussed.

2. The need for a standard occupational classification

A standard occupational classification is needed in official statistics in order to understand and monitor the contribution of human resources to the national economy. A key attribute of employed persons is occupational skills; these are acquired partly through formal qualification, but largely through work experience.

This being so, there is a demand from government agencies and others for a classification in which occupations are grouped according to the type and level of skill which they require. When applied to the economically active population (i.e. those who are in or are seeking employment) this enables the stock of occupational skills to be estimated, areas of shortage or over-provision to be identified, and the structure and functioning of the economy to be better understood. Analysis of the workforce by occupation and industry is a fundamental requirement of labour market intelligence and planning.

Similar demands for consistent occupational classification and statistics arise from such activities as vocational guidance and job placement.

A detailed classification of occupations is also required for analysing occupational health. For a century or more, disease, fertility and mortality rates have been derived by relating occupational data obtained from censuses of population to data derived from the registration of births and deaths and the notification of diseases.

Occupational information also provides the basis for several widely-used methods of socio-economic classification. The theme central to all of these classifications is that a person's occupation is one of the best available indicators of his or her position in society, whether conceived in terms of relation to the means of production, position in the labour market, or ranking according to prestige, status, or economic resources. This area of application generates a demand both for a standardised basic system of occupational classification and for a standardised method of inferring socio-economic status from occupation.

3. Concepts, applications, and data

SOC is designed to satisfy, as far as is practicable, all the above demands in the context of British society. Its development took account of the needs for the method of classification to recognise relevant and useful distinctions between occupational groups, to be standard as between applications, and to be as up-to-date as possible.

It is intended to apply to all the main official sources of occupational information. These include: the answers supplied by household form-fillers to questions in the Census of Population; information supplied by persons registering births, marriages, or deaths; responses given to questions included in social surveys; and administrative data relating to employment and vacancies. Previous experience suggests that a system suitable for these uses will also satisfy the needs of many other collectors and users of occupational information.

'Occupations' are viewed in SOC as coherent sets of work activities carried on by individuals. In defining occupational groups the aim has been to distinguish as far as possible in terms of the type and level of skills required to carry out the main work activities (see also the Introduction to SOC Volume 1).

A basic convention used in applying SOC, like other systems of occupational classification, is that a single employment contract is deemed to involve one occupation only. Thus a person employed as, say, a driver/receptionist is classified as either a driver or as a receptionist, according to which group of work activities predominates. The assumption involved is clearly a simplification of reality - and possibly a distortion from the point of view of some applications of the classification.

In everyday speech the key word used to refer to the work a person does tends to be 'job' rather than 'occupation'. Thus the key source of information in practical applications of SOC is the name of the person's job. The indispensable tool needed to classify occupations is a well-organised and comprehensive index of job titles (e.g. see SOC Volume 2). A consequence of this fundamental reliance upon job titles supplied by members of the public is that the way in which job titles are used in common parlance sets limits to the degree of detail, consistency, and reliability which can be achieved by the classification.

The SOC structure and coding index have been designed to be usable where those applying the classification have access only to information on the title and (preferably) the main work activity or activities associated with the job to be classified. In the majority of cases no other information is needed to code occupation. However, in certain cases accuracy and consistency of classification can be improved by using information about qualifications, industrial category and size of employing establishment, or status in employment. Such information is often available in sources such as the Census of Population and social surveys. Broadly speaking, it comes into play where the given job title and description of activities are not specific enough for coding purposes and further inferences must be made.

The use of ancillary information for SOC occupational coding is explained in the Introduction to SOC Volume 1 and in more detail in the Introduction to SOC Coding Index (Volume 2). A clear distinction should be made between this and the systematic use made of extra information on status in employment and size of employing establishment in deriving the Social Class and Socio-economic Groups classifications from the detailed occupational classification. This is further discussed at Section 6.3 below.

What has been said so far applies to the coding of occupational information supplied by members of the public without probing by an interviewer, for example as responses on census forms. Where information is obtained directly from job-holders by persons with specialist knowledge, for example in vocational guidance and job placement, it will often be possible to achieve more precise, detailed, and accurate classification.

The SOC structure, as set out in SOC Volume 1, is not geared to classification below the Occupational Unit Group level. In this respect SOC differs from CODOT, which provided for classification down to a more detailed '4-digit' level. However, the information on the content of occupational groups also provided in SOC Volume 1 will help those with more detailed classificatory needs and data sources to devise breakdowns suited to their own purposes below the Occupational Unit Group level, but still within the broader SOC structure.

4. Developing the SOC structure of classification*

SOC was designed to provide a single standard system of classification and at the same time to update and modernise the classificatory approach. However, its development depended heavily on what had gone before.

4.1 Relation of SOC to CO80, CODOT, and ISCO 88

SOC had two immediate 'parents' which contributed fundamentally to its development. One of these was the OPCS Classification of Occupations 1980 (CO80). This was the latest in a series of classifications, each a revision of its predecessor, which had been used over the years to code occupations in census, vital registration, and social survey applications. CO80 is the basis of occupational coding and hence also of socio-economic classification (see Sections 6.3 and 6.4) in, for example, the Labour Force Surveys, the General Household Survey, and many other surveys carried on both inside and outside government.

The second 'parent' of SOC was the Classification of Occupations and Directory of Occupational Titles (CODOT), published in 1972 and subsequently revised piecemeal. CODOT and its derivatives

---

* In this and the following sections the reader may find it useful to refer to the list of technical terms and definitions provided in Appendix C.

have been widely used by the Employment Departments for matching applicants to jobs in terms of skills and experience and also for statistical purposes. The KOS and Condensed KOS classifications (see below and Appendix C), which are derived from CODOT, have been used in coding occupational data from the New Earnings Survey and other surveys of employment.

A fuller account of the rather complicated situation, with respect to classification of occupations in official statistical sources, which existed in Great Britain before SOC was developed can be found in Thomas and Elias (1989), *Population Trends,* No. 55, OPCS.

Also relevant to the development of SOC was the simultaneous redevelopment of the International Standard Classification of Occupations (for more on ISCO 88 see Section 8). ISCO is not directly used in this country, but there is increasing pressure from the European Community and elsewhere for countries to provide occupational and other statistics harmonised to an international standard; and work is in progress to create such a standard based on ISCO 88. In developing SOC account was therefore taken of the ISCO 88 approach and some adjustments to the structure were made to improve compatibility.

4.2 Defining the SOC Occupational Unit Groups

The SOC structure of classificatory groups is set out in detail in SOC Volume 1. For convenience, however, Figure 1 opposite summarises it down to Minor Group level so as to give an overview of the classification. Figure 2 provides a schematic comparison of the old (pre-SOC) and SOC classificatory approaches. A reference list of terms and concepts introduced in this and following sections will be found at Appendix C.

The process of defining the SOC structure at the most detailed level of Occupational Unit Groups (OUGs) started in practice from the set of 350 'Operational Coding Groups' (OCGs) into which occupations were classified in CO80. All the CO80 Operational Coding Groups were thoroughly reviewed, taking account of: the principles of classification adopted; precedents in CODOT; the need to reflect the changing employment structure of Great Britain; and the perceived need to improve discrimination of occupations in certain areas of employment (e.g. jobs done mainly by women). User representative groups were consulted about parts of the classification in which they had special interest and knowledge.

For some 1980 OCGs no change of definition was thought necessary; others were split by introducing new distinctions. In certain cases it was decided to redistribute occupations which had formed the whole or parts of several OCGs in CO80 over several newly defined SOC OUGs.

In carrying out this revision an implicit general judgement and many specific judgements were made about the level of detail which should be aimed at in distinguishing basic occupational groups. An immensely detailed classification is too unwieldy for descriptive and statistical purposes and runs the risk of enshrining distinctions where there are no real differences from the point of view of many users. Also, it is subtly distorting to go down to fine detail in just those parts of the classification where that is technically possible, even though in reality there may be just as much differentiation between jobs in other areas. On the other hand, where real differences do exist and reliable distinctions can be made in terms of type of work and level of skill, a finer classification gives more scope, for example, to studies of gender segregation in employment or occupational mortality rates.

Judgements were also required about the degree of homogeneity which should be aimed at in placing jobs with different titles in the same occupational group. Such judgements had to be made in the light of very imperfect empirical knowledge of exactly what job activities underlie each job title in use.

Figure 1 The Definition of Sub-major Groups and Constituent Minor Groups

Major Group	Sub-major Groups	Constituent Minor Groups
1 Managers and Administrators	a) Corporate Managers and Administrators	10,11,12,13,14,15,19
	b) Managers/Proprietors in Agriculture and Services	16,17
2 Professional Occupations	a) Science and Engineering Professionals	20,21
	b) Health Professionals	22
	c) Teaching Professionals	23
	d) Other Professional Occupations	24,25,26,27,29
3 Associate Professional and Technical Occupations	a) Science and Engineering Associate Professionals	30,31,32
	b) Health Associate Professionals	34
	c) Other Associate Professional Occupations	33,35,36,37,38,39
4 Clerical and Secretarial Occupations	a) Clerical Occupations	40,41,42,43,44,49
	b) Secretarial Occupations	45,46
5 Craft and Related Occupations	a) Skilled Construction Trades	50
	b) Skilled Engineering Trades	51,52
	c) Other Skilled Trades	53,54,55,56,57,58,59
6 Personal and Protective Service Occupations	a) Protective Service Occupations	60,61
	b) Personal Service Occupations	62,63,64,65,66,67,69
7 Sales Occupations	a) Buyers, Brokers and Sales Reps.	70,71
	b) Other Sales Occupations	72,73,79
8 Plant and Machine Operatives	a) Industrial Plant and Machine Operators, Assemblers	80,81,82,83,84,85,86,89
	b) Drivers and Mobile Machine Operators	87,88
9 Other Occupations	a) Other Occupations in Agriculture, Forestry and Fishing	90
	b) Other Elementary Occupations	91,92,93,94,95,99

Figure 2 Present systems of occupational classification compared with the Standard Occupational Classification

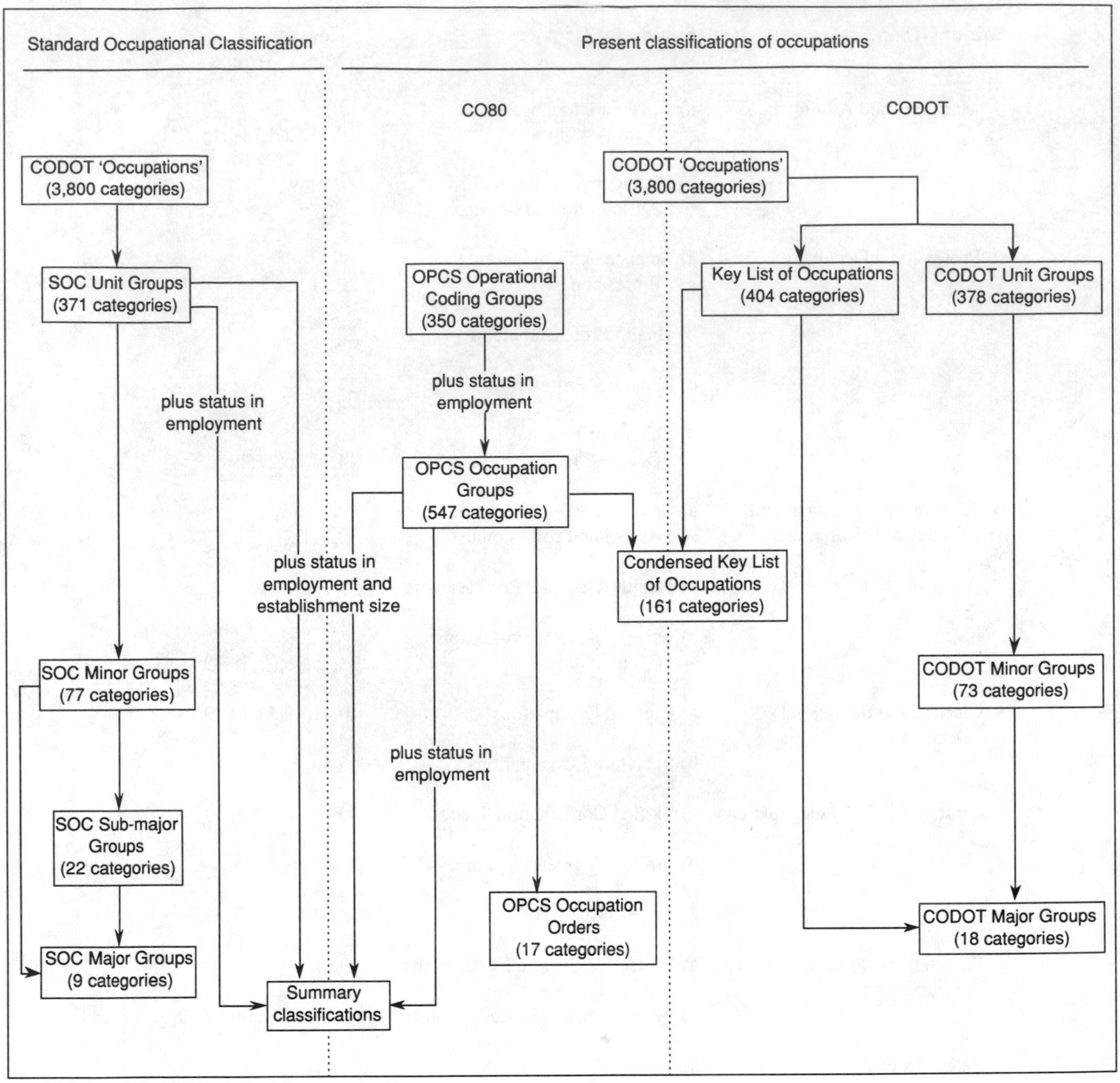

The outcome of this process was the new SOC system, comprising 371 Occupational Unit Groups, which replaced the 350 Operational Coding Groups in CO80 at the most detailed level of classification. This level of detail was also roughly comparable to that of the 3-digit occupational groups distinguished in CODOT.

In SOC there is no equivalent to the more detailed classification below the 3-digit level offered by CODOT. However, descriptions of work activities, occupational terms, and occupational skills associated with each SOC OUG are provided in the SOC documentation (see SOC Volume 1). These have been largely derived, with review and updating, from the corresponding parts of CODOT, but are rather less detailed.

4.3 Treatment of supervisory status in SOC

In CO80 the most detailed occupational categories (unit groups) used in presenting results were derived by splitting a number of OCGs to distinguish those jobs with and those jobs without supervisory status. Thus for example, foremen plumbers were assigned to a different unit group from other plumbers working as employees. This increased the number of occupational categories distinguished to 547 and was done to improve compatibility with CODOT, which in many places distinguishes supervisors.

In developing SOC an early decision was needed on whether to follow CODOT and CO80 in building this distinction between jobs with and without supervisory status into the basic occupational classification. After consideration it was decided that it would be more useful to focus the occupational classification as such exclusively on job activities and the nature and level of the job skills which they implied and to treat 'status in employment' as a dimension separate from 'occupation'.

As previously, the supervisor/non-supervisor distinction is invoked in deriving socio-economic classifications from the basic occupational classification (see Section 6.3 below).

4.4 Treatment of managerial jobs in SOC

An apparent exception to the general SOC principle of ignoring status in employment is the treatment of occupations referred to by job titles which include the word 'manager'. For most such occupations the assumption made in SOC is that 'managing' is the central work skill and activity. A Major, Minor, and Unit Group structure was accordingly developed to accommodate such managerial occupations in SOC.

4.5 Method of testing proposed new distinctions for practicability

A constraining influence in the development of SOC was the need to ensure that reliable distinctions between categories could be made on the basis of the raw data provided by censuses etc. Other proposed distinctions, however useful in theory, had to be rejected as impracticable.

The empirical base used for testing this was a one half percent systematic sample of verbatim and coded responses (approximately 115,000 cases in all) to questions on occupation and related topics asked in the 1981 Census of England and Wales. Each new distinction proposed was tested by applying it to relevant cases drawn from this census-derived database. Assessment was then made, first, of whether the information needed to make the distinction could be extracted from all or nearly all of the census responses; and second, of whether the allocation of cases to new categories both seemed to be plausible and was consistent with other information present in the database (e.g. qualifications, industry, etc.).

In certain cases, where changes in job technology and nomenclature had been very rapid during the nineteen eighties, recourse was had to other sources, such as job vacancy listings provided by the Employment Service and the trade press, to test whether proposed distinctions appeared workable.

4.6 Higher order grouping of occupations in SOC

There are many applications which require a more summary level of classification derived by aggregation from the basic Unit Groups. SOC follows CODOT and ISCO in having an explicitly hierarchical structure to answer this need.

Two levels of aggregation above the basic Unit Group level are directly recognised in SOC: the Major Groups (of which there are 9), the Minor Groups (77), and the Unit Groups (371). These levels are indexed respectively by the first, the first two, and all three digits of the SOC OUG number. At a late stage in the development of SOC it was decided to follow the new International Standard Classification of Occupations (ISCO 88 - see Section 8 below) in proposing a further level of aggregation intermediate between Major and Minor Groups. This yields the Sub-major Groups, of which there are 22. (For fuller explanation see the Introduction to SOC Volume 1. Appendix C of the present volume provides an aide-memoire.)

At the Minor Group level of classification the general principle is to distinguish occupations by type, rather than by level, of skill. At this level some superficial similarities to classification by industry appear in SOC. This is inevitable, because similarities between occupations in terms of work activities and work skills are often inferred by reference to materials worked with and equipment used, which in turn may be characteristic of particular industries. Nevertheless, SOC is unambiguously a classification of occupations, consistently maintaining the conceptual distinction between industry and occupation which has been gradually clarified over a century and a half in this country.

At the Sub-major and Major Group levels of SOC it was found most relevant and useful to distinguish groups by a mixture of 'type of skill' and 'level of skill' criteria. The level of skill demanded by an occupation is clearly an important criterion; but in practice the link between occupational title and implied level of skill cannot be pressed too far. In terms of levels of education and length of training, many jobs have similar requirements, and, beyond that, no agreed rationale exists for equating levels of skill in quite different areas, such as, say, shop retailing and plumbing. A higher-level classification focusing entirely on level of skill would in any case have little practical application because of the segmentation of the employment market in terms of type of skill.

It is important to remember that SOC focuses throughout on work skills and activities and does not at any level recognise other distinctions, such as between employees and the self-employed, or between employees with and without formal supervisory status.

4.7 Higher order grouping based on CO80

Figure 2 in Section 4.2 shows how the hierarchical structure of SOC as just described replaces a less integrated system for higher order classification based on CO80. In the case of CO80 this need was supplied by the 17 Occupational Orders (see *Classification of Occupations 1980* pp xiv-xxix). These were formed by aggregating CO80 OCGs, though as a classification the Occupational Orders predate CO80. Some of them broadly resemble SOC Major or Sub-major Groups, others are similar to Socio-economic Groups (see Section 6.3 below). Occupational Orders have been quite widely used in statistical applications, but it is expected that they will be superseded by the higher order classifications offered by SOC.

Reference was made at Section 4.1 above to Condensed KOS. Although this effectively grouped the 350 CO80 Operational Coding Groups into 161 categories, it was not designed as a summary level of classification in the same sense as, say, SOC Minor Groups, but rather as a 'bridge' between CO80 and CODOT. As such it has been widely used, and Section 6.2 below discusses the effects of rebasing Condensed KOS on SOC.

A summary six-fold classification, formed by aggregation from Condensed KOS, has also been used in the Employment Departments, but it is expected that this will be superseded by SOC Major Groups.

8

5. Continuity between SOC and CO80 at Unit Group level

For analytic purposes which involve comparisons over time, it is highly desirable that the framework of comparison be kept constant, so that changes in the real world are not confounded with changes in the frame through which it is viewed. However, this principle must not be pressed too far. Few would wish occupational coding in the 1991 Census to be based on the classification and instructions used by coders on the 1911 Census, even if that were operationally possible. Social and technological change blurs old distinctions or makes them irrelevant and calls for new occupations to be recognised and new distinctions between occupational groups to be made.

Hence every revision of the existing classification of occupations requires a balance to be struck between the needs to be up-to-date and relevant to current requirements, on the one hand, and to preserve continuity with what has gone before, on the other. This general judgement then has to be implemented through a large number of detailed decisions affecting continuity with previous classifications and compatibility with other current systems. The basic dilemma can never be entirely avoided, though in some applications special measures may be taken to reduce the immediate disruptive effects of discontinuity (see Section 8 below).

In the following sections we discuss indicators of continuity and compatibility for statistical purposes and use them to measure the degree of discontinuity between SOC and CO80 at the most detailed level of classification. We then go on to discuss the rebasing of existing summary and socio-economic classifications on SOC and the implications of that for continuity of classification in each case.

5.1 Defining and measuring continuity of classification

There is no straightforward, generally applicable way of resolving issues of continuity and discontinuity in classifying occupations. Changing a classification is bound to cause some problems to the analyst when presenting or analysing data on trends over time. However, there are often very real, though less obvious, problems in making no change, since the world described by the classification is itself changing. Not only do entirely new occupations come into being, but occupational groups which formerly contained predominantly skilled occupations may become progressively deskilled, even though the formal definition of the group in terms of job titles assigned to it remains the same. A researcher who thinks he or she is comparing like with like over time will be misled. If the content of the group in terms of job titles is deliberately changed in revising the classification so as to exclude occupations judged to be deskilled, real consistency may be improved for analytic purposes, even though formally discontinuity has been introduced.

As regards the measurement of continuity/discontinuity, a crude measure of formal continuity is given by the proportion of basic classificatory groups in the 'new' classification (SOC OUGs) which correspond, one-to-one, to groups in the 'old' classification (CO80 OCGs). However, some occupational groups contain much higher proportions of the total population of jobs (as reflected in the 1981 Census subsample) than others. It is therefore more meaningful to take as the measure of continuity the proportion of the reference population which falls into groups which correspond in the two classifications.

For some purposes one might wish to count as instances of correspondence cases where two or more OUGs, when combined together, correspond to one OCG; or where combining several OCGs produces a group corresponding exactly to one OUG. However, once groups have to be combined to give correspondence it is likely that distinctions of interest to some analysts will be lost.

5.2 Continuity between SOC Unit Groups and CO80 Operational Coding Groups

Table 1 (see page 29) shows the degree of continuity between the SOC Unit Groups and the CO80 Operational Coding Groups according to the criteria described above. The population proportions were estimated by reference to a systematic one half percent sample of occupations drawn from the 1981 Census returns.

Direct one-to-one correspondence is preserved for groups containing only about 56% of the 1981 reference population; while 38% of the population fell into OCGs which could not be directly matched in SOC. The latter proportion falls somewhat if 'near-matches' and aggregations are allowed, but is still very substantial.

The main conclusion to be drawn from Table 1 is that, for analysts interested in a range of occupational groups at the most detailed level, the degree of discontinuity between SOC and CO80 is large enough to make direct comparisons at OCG/OUG level at best problematic and at worst impossible. However, Section 9 below describes measures which will mitigate the effects of discontinuity in certain official statistical sources. At more summary levels of classification the discontinuity is much less serious, as shown in Section 6.

6. Summary and derived classifications based on SOC

While SOC itself offers a number of different levels of classification, many users have a commitment to summary and derived classifications based on CO80, for which SOC itself does not provide an exact replacement.

The summary and derived classifications of this kind which have most frequently been used in official statistics and elsewhere are: Condensed KOS; Social Class based on Occupation (Registrar General's Social Class); and Socio-economic Groups.

6.1 The maximum-continuity rule

In Section 5 it was pointed out that in updating classifications we cannot avoid choices between adjusting to change and preserving continuity. In developing SOC itself adjusting to change was an important criterion, but in rebasing the summary classifications on SOC the aim has been to maximise formal continuity, in the sense of maximising the proportion of jobs (and hence persons) in the reference population which will be allocated to the same Condensed KOS, Social Class, or SEG category when these classifications are based on SOC as they were when they were based on CO80.

The alternative course would be to break formal continuity and adjust the method of aggregating occupational groups to form summary classifications, taking account of perceived changes in the way occupation is related to the social and economic position of persons and households. There is a case for doing that but it raises some difficult issues, which OPCS hopes to address in a separate initiative (see Section 7 below). In the meantime it was felt that tinkering with the summary classifications would cause more problems than it solved.

In practice preserving formal continuity of the summary classifications presents no problem where all the occupations allocated to a given SOC Occupational Unit Group were, under CO80, assigned to the same summary category - the same Social Class, say. In such situations all the occupations in question can be and are allocated to the same Social Class under SOC as under CO80.

10

Approximation is necessary only when a single SOC OUG contains occupations which, when the summary classifications were based on CO80, were assigned to different summary categories. Where this occurs, the rule has been to allocate the whole SOC OUG to that summary category to which the greatest number of constituent cases were assigned under CO80 (using the 1981 Census returns as the reference population).

Thus for example, if a single SOC OUG contains 7,000 cases which, under CO80, were assigned to Social Class IV Manual and 23,000 cases which were allocated to Social Class V, then under SOC the whole of the OUG is allocated to Social Class V. The corollary of this is, of course, that the 7,000 former Social Class IV Manual cases will be allocated to a different Social Class under SOC (i.e. Social Class V) from the one they were allocated to under CO80 (i.e. Social Class IV) and will contribute to the overall measure of discontinuity.

6.2 Condensed KOS

The Condensed KOS classification of 161 categories was formed by aggregating the OCGs identified in the 1980 classification up to a point where they could be matched by aggregating CODOT categories. It therefore provided a link between the two classifications for statistical purposes. While serving that purpose, it was a reflection of the imperfect assimilation between CO80 and CODOT now superseded by SOC. Condensed KOS has been used in a number of statistical and analytical applications.

Table 2 (see page 30) shows how accurately Condensed KOS, as derived from CO80, can be matched by aggregating SOC Unit Groups. A tabulation of the two versions of Condensed KOS one against the other is too large and diffuse to present, so instead Table 2 shows net percentage change in the number of cases assigned to each Condensed KOS category, due to rebasing on SOC. For many categories there is no change, but for a few the number of cases changes by 60% or more. Since the maximum continuity rule has been followed, this is the closest approximation that can be achieved on the basis of SOC. As in the case of with Unit Groups, this degree of discontinuity will have a serious effect on some types of analysis. More detailed information can be obtained from the OPCS Occupational Information Unit (see Appendix B).

6.3 Socio-economic classifications based on occupation

A large group of users of occupation-based statistics and of occupational coding procedures are interested not in the detailed levels of the occupational classification, but in the socio-economic classifications derived from it. In Great Britain two such classifications have been widely used in official statistics, namely: Social Class based on Occupation (Registrar General's Social Class); and Socio-economic Groups. These are generally referred to below as SC and SEG; the titles and definitions of the categories used are set out in Figure 3 and Figure 4 respectively.

Occupation is not the only indicator of socio-economic status which can be used, and it may not be the best for all purposes. However, there is some consensus that, within the range of individual and household-level variables typically available from censuses and other sources in Great Britain, occupation has proved robust as a marker variable for socio-economic position. It is therefore likely that occupation-referenced methods of assessing socio-economic status will continue in use.

To derive a socio-economic classification from occupation, rules are needed to relate occupation to socio-economic position and to specify when and how ancillary information, for example on status in employment, should be used. Rules for doing this were defined for CO80 and set out in *Classification of Occupations 1980*, Appendix B.

11

Figure 3 Social Class based on Occupation

Since the 1911 Census it has been customary for certain analytical purposes, to arrange the large number of groups of the occupational classification into a small number of broad categories called Social Classes. It has recently been decided to extend the title of the classification to 'Social Class based on Occupation' and change the name of Class II from 'Intermediate' to 'Managerial and Technical'.

The categories are as follows:

I	Professional, etc. occupations
II	Managerial and Technical occupations
III	Skilled occupations
	(N) non-manual
	(M) manual
IV	Partly skilled occupations
V	Unskilled occupations

The occupation groups included in each of these categories have been selected in such a way as to bring together, as far as possible, people with similar levels of occupational skill. In general, each occupation group is assigned as a whole to one or other social class and no account is taken of differences between individuals in the same occupation group, for example, differences in education. However, for persons having the employment status of foreman or manager the following additional rules apply:

(a) each occupation is given a basic social class;

(b) persons of foreman status whose basic social class is IV or V are allocated to Social Class III;

(c) persons of manager status are allocated to Social Class II with certain exceptions.

Figure 4 Socio-economic Groups

Classification by Socio-economic Groups was introduced in 1951 and extensively amended in 1961. The classification aims to bring together people with jobs of similar social and economic status. The allocation of occupied persons to Socio-economic Groups is determined by considering their employment status and occupation (and industry, though for practical purposes no direct reference is made since it is possible in Great Britain to use classification by occupation as a means of distinguishing effectively those engaged in agriculture).

The Socio-economic Groups with brief definitions are:

(1) Employers and managers in central and local government, industry, commerce, etc. - large establishments

> 1.1 Employers in industry, commerce, etc.
> Persons who employ others in non-agricultural enterprises employing 25 or more persons.

> 1.2 Managers in central and local government, industry, commerce, etc.
> Persons who generally plan and supervise in non-agricultural enterprises employing 25 or more persons.

(2) Employers and managers in industry, commerce, etc. - small establishments

> 2.1 Employers in industry, commerce, etc. - small establishments. As in 1.1 but in establishments employing fewer than 25 persons.

> 2.2 Managers in industry, commerce, etc. - small establishments. As in 1.2 but in establishments employing fewer than 25 persons.

(3) Professional workers - self-employed

Self-employed persons engaged in work normally requiring qualifications of university degree standard.

(4) Professional workers - employees

Employees engaged in work normally requiring qualifications of university degree standard.

(5) Intermediate non-manual workers

> 5.1 Ancillary workers and artists
> Employees engaged in non-manual occupations ancillary to the professions, not normally requiring qualifications of university degree standard; persons engaged in artistic work and not employing others therein. Self-employed nurses, medical auxiliaries, teachers, work study engineers and technicians are included.

> 5.2 Foremen and supervisors non-manual
> Employees (other than managers) engaged in occupations included in group 6, who formally and immediately supervise others engaged in such occupations.

13

Figure 4 - *continued*

(6)   **Junior non-manual workers**

Employees, not exercising general planning or supervisory powers, engaged in clerical, sales and non-manual communications occupations, excluding those who have additional and formal supervisory functions (these are included in group 5.2).

(7)   **Personal service workers**

Employees engaged in service occupations caring for food, drink, clothing and other personal needs.

(8)   **Foremen and supervisors - manual**

Employees (other than managers) who formally and immediately supervise others engaged in manual occupations, whether or not themselves engaged in such occupations.

(9)   **Skilled manual workers**

Employees engaged in manual occupations which require considerable and specific skills.

(10) **Semi-skilled manual workers**

Employees engaged in manual occupations which require slight but specific skills.

(11) **Unskilled manual workers**

Other employees engaged in manual occupations.

(12) **Own account workers (other than professional)**

Self-employed persons engaged in any trade, personal service or manual occupation not normally requiring training of university degree standard and having no employees other than family workers.

(13) **Farmers - employers and managers**

Persons who own, rent or manage farms, market gardens or forests, employing people other than family workers in the work of the enterprise.

(14) **Farmers - own account**

Persons who own or rent farms, market gardens or forests and having no employees other than family workers.

(15) **Agricultural workers**

Persons engaged in tending crops, animals, game or forests, or operating agricultural or forestry machinery.

(16) **Members of armed forces**

(17) **Inadequately described and not stated occupations**

Many (though not all) users of the socio-economic classifications are mainly concerned to avoid discontinuity. Using the maximum-continuity principle explained at Section 6.1 it has been possible to update the 1980 rules and rebase them on SOC at the price of only a modest amount of discontinuity (see Section 6.4). The new conventions are set out in detail in Table A1 of Appendix A.

The principle of preserving maximum continuity with the 1980 versions of the classifications will govern the production of SOC-based official statistics bearing on socio-economic status up to the mid-nineteen nineties. This includes output from the 1991 Census. Census output will also offer statistics based on SOC Major, Sub-major, and Minor Groups. Some discussion of the broader issues raised by application of the socio-economic classifications will be found at Section 7 below.

6.4 Social Class based on Occupation and Socio-economic Groups: continuity

In Table 3 Social Class as based on CO80 is tabulated against Social Class as rebased on SOC and in Table 4 Socio-economic Groups as based on CO80 are tabulated against Socio-economic Groups as rebased on SOC, in each case using the one half percent subsample of occupations drawn from the 1981 Census returns (See pages 34 and 35).

The most salient net effects on the distribution of the sample by Social Class are: a decrease from 18.0% to 16.8% in the proportion of cases assigned to Social Class IV; and an increase from 6.2% to 7.6% in the proportion of cases assigned to Social Class V.

The most salient net effects on the distribution of the sample by SEG are: a decrease from 5.4% to 4.0% in the proportion of cases assigned to SEG 7 'Personal service workers'; and an increase from 6.0% to 7.5% in the proportion of cases assigned to SEG 11 'Unskilled manual workers'. The main source of this net shift is a gross reassignment of 1.3% of the sample from SEG 7 to SEG 11. This reflects a change in the treatment of 'domestic' and 'cleaning' occupations which also contributed to the net shift from Social Class IV to Social Class V and is discussed more fully below.

While the net redistribution of cases forced by rebasing on SOC is quite small relative to the total population, the impact on Social Class V and SEGs 7 and 11, which are small categories dispropor-tionately affected, is considerable.

An overall measure of gross discontinuity between 'old' and rebased classifications is given by the proportions of cases falling into off-diagonal cells of Tables 3 and 4. For Social Class the proportion of all cases which fall in off-diagonal cells is 2.3% and for SEG 2.0%. In each table just one off-diagonal cell accounts for more than half of all the observed discontinuity. This is the transfer of cases from Social Class IV to Social Class V and from SEG 7 to SEG 11. These transfers both result from the different treatment in CO80 and in SOC of the job-titles 'Domestic (helper in school, hospital, private home etc.)' and 'Cleaner (domestic or not elsewhere classified)'. In CO80 these occupations were not only distinguished as separate OCGs but were also allocated to different Social Classes and SEGs. The former were assigned to SC IV 'Partly skilled occupations' and SEG 7 'Personal service workers'; and the latter to SC V 'Unskilled occupations' and SEG 11 'Unskilled manual workers'.

In constructing SOC it became clear, after careful scrutiny of the content of the categories by reference to the 1981 subsample database, that the job-titles 'Domestic' and 'Cleaner' were often used interchangeably, that the dominant work activity in either case was 'cleaning', rather than 'personal care', and that distinguishing the two was not justified. Accordingly jobs of these types were placed in a single SOC OUG '958 Cleaners, domestics' (see SOC Volume 1).

In rebasing Social Class and Socio-economic Groups on SOC the maximum continuity rule was then invoked. Since the majority of the cases allocated to OUG 958 were 'cleaners' who had been assigned to SC V and SEG 11, the whole of OUG 958 was now assigned to SC V/SEG 11, including the 'domestics' who had formerly, when separately distinguished under CO80, been assigned to SC IV and SEG 7. In this case the workings of the rule seem quite justifiable on substantive, as well as maximum continuity grounds; since the work activities characterising SOC OUG 958 involve the lowest level of skill and training and therefore properly belong in SC V/SEG 11 'Unskilled occupations'/'Unskilled manual workers'. This is consistent with their allocation to SOC Major Group 9.

Analysis by gender, using the 1981 database, showed that the 'domestic' jobs which are differently treated in SOC and in CO80 were in the vast majority of cases done by women. A high proportion were also part-time jobs. The proportion of women's jobs reassigned from SC IV to SC V was thus 3.5%, whereas the proportion of men's jobs reassigned was 0.2%. For analysts whose focus is on women's employment, therefore, the discontinuity caused by rebasing on SOC is greater than suggested by Tables 3 and 4; but for analysis where the reference is to men's jobs the discontinuity is less than suggested.

This particular change may appear to run counter to the stated SOC aim of discriminating more finely between different kinds of jobs done predominantly by women than was done in CO80. This aim has been pursued with some success elsewhere in SOC, for example in the treatment of clerical/secretarial, nursing, and teaching occupations (see SOC Volume 1). In those cases it was judged that real differences in work activities and skills existed and should be brought out wherever that could be done reliably. However, attempting to preserve a distinction which does not correspond to real differences in work content could serve no useful analytic purpose, but would merely disguise the degree of concentration of women's jobs (and particularly part-time jobs) in certain low-skilled areas.

It should also be noted that in many applications the allocation of individuals to Social Classes or Socio-economic Groups is done by reference to the occupation of a household reference person (see Section 7.4). The rules normally used in censuses and surveys to identify the household reference person have the effect of selecting a male in the majority of cases. Part of the justification for this is that it avoids allocating socio-economic status on the basis of jobs held (often part-time) by married or cohabiting women, which in certain applications could produce misleading results. Where socio-economic classification is done on the basis of the occupation of a household reference person as conventionally defined, the degree of discontinuity caused by rebasing on SOC will be significantly less than suggested by Tables 3 and 4.

In general it is thought that the relatively low level of discontinuity in the SC and SEG classifications which results from rebasing on SOC will not cause distortions intolerable to the majority of users interested in tracking real change in the distributions over time. It contrasts with the much greater degree of discontinuity at the OCG/OUG level indicated by Table 1 and shows that most changes between CO80 and SOC were within, rather than across, the boundaries of Social Classes and Socio-economic Groups.

7. Some issues in the application of socio-economic classifications based on occupation

Socio-economic classification raises a wider set of conceptual and technical issues than does the occupational classification on which it is often based. Some of the main ones are the following:

- What should be the rationale and method for determining where, in the scheme of socio-economic classification, holders of a particular occupation are to be placed? On what basis should such allocations be revised and updated?

- What are the theoretical and practical implications of the fact that some data sources are of poorer quality than others and/or may not include all the information strictly required to assign a socio-economic status?

- How should a person's socio-economic position be defined and measured - for example should it be by reference to his or her current occupation, main lifetime occupation, or what? How should those who are not currently employed, or who have never been employed, be treated?

- When should a person's socio-economic position be defined by reference to his or her own occupation and when by reference to the occupation of some other member of his or her family or household (or that of his or her parents)? How should a household reference person be chosen?

During the period following the 1991 Census OPCS hopes to be able to sponsor a review of socio-economic classifications, taking account of the needs of different groups of users. It is hoped to address some or all of the above issues and to find a generally acceptable method of revising and up-dating the socio-economic classifications used in official statistical sources.

In the meantime it may be worth briefly discussing each of the issues listed above, indicating what the obstacles are to resolving them straightforwardly and what the implications and consequences of different practices might be.

7.1 Rationales for developing and updating occupation-referenced socio-economic classifications

The two occupation-based socio-economic classifications used in official statistics, Social Classes and Socio-economic Groups, are widely used and provide long time series. There is therefore always a strong lobby for their continuation in their existing form with minimum formal discontinuity. However, questions and doubts have often been raised.

One issue is, whether the cost and complication of maintaining two different summary, occupation-referenced socio-economic measures is justified, given that they often seem to serve similar analytic needs in practice, even though historically created for different purposes.

Aside from that, the rationale and conventions, according to which SC and SEG are derived from occupation and status in employment, have often been challenged. Not only the details of the 1980 derivation conventions (which were mainly inherited from earlier versions), but also the lack of clearly stated principles underpinning them have been criticised from a theoretical viewpoint.

Some critics have argued that SC and SEG should be supplemented or replaced by alternative occupation-referenced measures, and differing theoretical views and practical needs have led to the development of other occupation-referenced scales as alternatives to SC or SEG. These are all ultimately based on some version of the official classification of occupations. They include various scales designed to measure social status or reflect social stratification which have been used mainly in academic research (e.g. the Hope-Goldthorpe and Cambridge Scales). They also include the Social Grades (A, B, C1, C2, D, E) popular in market research, though in practice two-stage coding via OPCS OUGs has generally been superseded by short-cut methods in which the commoner occupational titles are directly assigned to Social Grades.

Experts differ widely on exactly how information on occupation (plus ancillary data) can best be used to derive useful socio-economic measures, but computer-assisted coding packages are now becoming available which enable researchers and others who have access to raw data and wish to derive any one of a range of socio-economic classifications to do so directly at the occupational coding stage.

Nevertheless, many analysts remain dependent upon official statistical sources which embody socio-economic measures as derived and promulgated by OPCS. Also, many practitioners of occupational classification will probably wish to continue following OPCS - and in particular Census of Population - practice as a standard. For both, updating and revision of the existing socio-economic classifications raises issues of continuity.

Most users are concerned about formal discontinuities resulting from revisions and updates. The rebasing of the two occupation-referenced socio-economic classifications used in official statistics on SOC does not lead to major formal discontinuities with the classifications based on CO80 (Section 6.4), but that is not the only issue. The conventions of classification cannot remain fixed once and for all. Change over time in the skill and activity content of occupations and/or in the relative status attached to them should be reflected by changing the allocation of occupations to socio-economic categories. Such changes should be justified by some demonstration that they tend to maintain the validity with which the underlying social dimension is measured over time.

7.2 Implications of poorer or less complete data

7.2.1 The Census of Population model

In the past OPCS has not given any explicit guidance on application issues, but has confined itself to providing a brief description of the socio-economic classifications plus practical information on how to derive them. The precedent implicit in such publication has generally been practice on the Census of Population. This is reasonable in the sense that the census gives complete and detailed coverage of all occupations and census results provide the most commonly used standard with which other researchers and analysts might wish to compare their results. In some cases, however, practice in vital registration or survey coding, if different, may be a more relevant model.

Relevant features of the methodology of the 1991 Census (which follows that of the 1981 and 1971 Censuses in most respects) are the following:

(a) Two questions are asked about the occupation of each member of a census household, one asking for a job title and the other for a description of main work tasks;

(b) Job titles are also used to establish whether or not the job done carries supervisory status (as indicated by terms such as 'foreman', 'supervisor', etc.);

(c) A further question is asked to establish other aspects of the person's status in employment and, in particular, whether or not he/she is self-employed;

(d) Questions are asked to establish the industrial sector to which the person's employing establishment should be allocated;

(e) Questions are asked to establish whether the person holds any recognised higher level (roughly, post GCE 'A' Level) qualification and, if so, in what subject(s) and at what level;

(f) Information is supplied by a household form-filler in answer to each of these questions; the form filler may or may not consult other household members in the course of completing the form;

(g) In order to economise on time and resources, only a random one in ten census forms are selected for occupational coding, and results for occupation and some other variables are therefore based on a 10% sample.

The coding of occupation depends in the vast majority of census cases only on the items of information obtained at (a). However, census coding practice aims to make the best use of relevant items of information which are available on the census form (within constraints imposed by the need to complete large amounts of coding rapidly and efficiently). Where the information at (a) is insufficient to establish unambiguously to which OUG the job belongs, recourse may be had to the information at (d) and very occasionally to the information at (b), (c), or (e). In order to derive the SC or SEG to which the person holding an occupation should be allocated, the information at (b) and (c) is formally required in a substantial proportion of cases, in addition to the OUG to which the relevant job has been allocated.

7.2.2 Reliability of census-style collection and coding of occupational information and of the derived socio-economic classifications

The results of Census post-enumeration checks suggested that in 1981 the reliability/validity of census coding of occupation at OUG level, as assessed by re-collecting the relevant information by interview and independently coding it, was around 75%. The reliability/validity of allocation of cases to Social Classes based on Occupation was around 87% and to Socio-economic Groups around 84%. (There is, of course, a general tendency for reliability to increase as the fineness of the distinctions called for decreases.)

These estimates of reliability/validity are not strictly comparable with estimates of coding consistency reported in the literature. Other tests suggest that the levels of coding consistency achieved in processing occupational information from the 1981 Census were around 90%. Further inconsistencies arose in the context of the post-enumeration check from the fact that the information was collected by different methods and sometimes from different persons (though about the same job) in census and follow-up survey; and that the coding was carried out by separate clerical coding units (though using the same classification).

It is unlikely that average consistency levels of census coding were much affected by the availability of information of types (b), (c), or (e) above. However, it is thought that these made a worthwhile contribution to the validity with which particular occupations were identified. The major contributors to inconsistency in census coding of occupation are thought to be: the vagueness or inadequacy of many of the job titles and job descriptions provided; and variability in the conclusions drawn by coders from such information.

7.2.3 Handling data from other sources

Basing the standard approach to socio-economic classification on census practice is a compromise position. On the one hand, the census is not as good a source of occupational and related data as, for example, purpose-designed interview surveys on which series of questions may be put to informants and inadequate answers may be probed by trained interviewers. On the other hand, much of the occupational data obtained through vital registration and administrative sources is scantier and of poorer quality than census data.

Imposing a system of occupational coding and socio-economic classification developed with the census in mind on other, more detailed, higher quality data sources does not present too many immediate practical problems. However, coding is sensitive to differences in the precise words used to describe occupations and in the ancillary data available, so the use of different data collection procedures inevitably leads to different occupational and socio-economic codes being assigned in a proportion of cases. Evidence from coding reliability checks suggests that the availability of fuller verbatim information may well improve the validity of coding in some cases, but does not automatically improve its consistency (reliability) and may even reduce it. For optimum coding reliability the ideal is for the informant to name an occupation very succinctly, using wording which occurs verbatim in the coding index.

Other sources present different problems. For example, the circumstances under which information on occupation and employment status is collected at death registration are heavily constrained. Information is often supplied by a person who is not very well informed about the deceased person's former occupation. It is not possible to collect census-style data of types (d) or (e); information of types (b) and (c) is often suspect or lacking; and even type (a) information is often of poorer quality than on the census.

In dealing with registration-type data it is necessary to supplement and modify census coding instructions with default rules for assigning a socio-economic status in cases where the information is vague or deficient. The price of doing this is inconsistency with the census which manifests itself, for example, in biases affecting the interpretation of mortality ratios for occupational groups or social classes where the census supplies the denominator and death registration the numerator. On the other hand, where coding to socio-economic categories is required only to provide a broad control variable this looseness matters less.

There is thus no wholly satisfactory way out of the dilemma presented by occupational data sources differing in quality and detail. The judgement made in constructing SOC and its OPCS predecessors has been that it is best to adopt census assumptions and to use the standard classification on data which are sometimes inadequate, than either to resort to a much less powerful classification which is adapted to poorer-quality data (but wastes better-quality data), or to give up altogether on occupational and socio-economic coding of registration and similar data.

7.3 Defining a reference occupation

Occupation is not a permanent attribute of individuals, like gender or date of birth. Some individuals have many different occupations during their working lives. In some cases this indicates career progression, in other cases not. Even if all studies involving attribution of socio-economic status to individuals were conducted post mortem and with perfect knowledge of each person's complete occupational career, there could be much scope for theoretical argument as to which occupation most validly indicated the person's socio-economic status for particular analytic purposes.

The issue of post mortem attribution of socio-economic status arises in principle in the case of analysis of death registration data. However, theoretical issues are largely pre-empted by the practical limitations of the information obtainable from informants. Whereas concepts such as 'main lifetime occupation' would be useful in theory, the rules needed to define such a concept and ensure that a 'main lifetime occupation' could always be identified in practice are too complicated. The concept aimed at is therefore 'last main paid occupation', but in some cases responses probably relate to some different occupation considered by the informant to be the deceased's 'real' occupation.

In the main run of applications of socio-economic classification in censuses and surveys, living individuals at any stage of their occupational careers may need to be assigned a socio-economic status. The rule generally applied is that the reference occupation for purposes of assigning a socio- economic status should be the the person's current occupation, if any; or, if currently not in paid employment, the most recent occupation.

This may be thought unsatisfactory, for example in the cases of currently employed persons whose current occupation is in some way atypical of their employment career and 'true' socio-economic status. For some applications it might be argued that those who are unemployed but seeking work, those who are permanently sick, those who are retired from paid employment, etc. should be assigned to separate categories. However, to do that would detract from comparability with other sources on the distribution socio-economic status.

The resolution of issues of this kind must depend on the intended purpose of analysis by socio-economic status. Consider the case of a person who was formerly a senior industrial manager, having reached that position by career progression, but has now retired and taken a part-time paid job as a book-keeper for a charity. If current conditions of employment (say) are to be analysed by socio-economic status, then the reference occupation for assigning socio-economic status should be the current job. On the other hand, if the variables to be analysed by socio-economic status relate to social and cultural background, income, or economic assets, then the former (full-time, well-pensioned) managerial job should ideally be taken as the basis for classification.

As in the case of death registration, the difficulty in the context of standardised data-collection operations is to recognise those cases where the current occupation might be regarded as 'misleading' for classificatory purposes and to provide rules which will lead in all cases and in a reliable and consistent way to a 'non-misleading' alternative. In practice the extra complication involved is seldom thought worthwhile.

Social Class and SEG are thus much more problematic variables than age or sex, even though they are often mentioned in the same breath as general purpose classifiers. The fact that it is relatively easy to collect information on occupation and the existence of rules for deriving socio-economic status should not blind the analyst to the crudeness and fallibility of underlying assumptions, or to the sources of unreliability mentioned at Section 7.2.2 above. The usefulness of socio-economic classification referenced to occupation depends on the strength and consistency of the correlation assumed to exist between occupation and the variable(s) of real interest to the analyst. In many situations, other more direct or less complicated methods of operationalising the required socio-economic variable may be preferable (see also Section 7.4 below).

7.4 Household reference persons

The problems so far discussed apply when the person to be assigned to a socio-economic category has a paid occupation to which reference can be made. However, a high proportion of adults and nearly all children under the age of sixteen in this country have no current paid occupation. For the retired and also the temporarily unemployed recourse is often had to the last (main) paid occupation, but even that does not work for those persons who have never had a paid occupation.

There are, moreover, many cases where assigning an individual a socio-economic status on the basis of his or her own current or past occupation seems misleading. The main reason for this is that most people live not as independent individuals, but as members of domestic groups - that is, households - which share both housing accommodation and socio-economic circumstances. A household member's own job may have relatively little influence in determining his or her socio-economic status. This applies particularly to young adults living in the parental home and to persons choosing to do less demanding or part-time jobs on the basis that another household member takes responsibility for bringing in most of the household's income. There are in fact good arguments for treating socio-economic status as fundamentally an attribute of households (or perhaps families) and only secondarily of their constituent members.

However, this argument has to be stood on its head if the method of assigning socio-economic status is to depend on occupation. In developed economies households as such cannot be said to have occupations, and to determine the socio-economic status of a household one must refer to the occupation(s) of one or several of its members. A simplified practical solution is then to select one member of the household as reference person and take that person's occupation and status in employment as the basis for determining the socio-economic status of the household as a whole, and hence of its other members. This solution has long been used in presenting the results of censuses and other social enquiries.

Two concepts have been influential in determining how to select a household reference person. The first is that of a 'chief economic supporter' of the household, interpreted as the household member contributing the largest amount of income to the household. The second concept is that of the 'householder' or 'head of household', who is (or was) assumed to represent the household in its socio-economic and other relationships with the outside world. In the nineteenth and earlier twentieth centuries these two concepts were assumed to identify the same person in the majority of cases. It seemed sensible, therefore, to treat this person as the reference person in assigning a socio-economic status to the household.

This basic approach is still followed in collecting and analysing many social data, though with refinements to the definitions where that is feasible (e.g. in social surveys) and often with an available alternative of assigning adults who have, or have had, paid employment a socio-economic status according to their own occupation.

To be useful in conducting censuses and surveys, the reference person concept needs to be operationalised through practical selection rules. Such rules must be simple and objective and their application must result in the unambiguous selection of a single reference person for each household. They must not require the eliciting and recording of complicated or sensitive information, or the making of potentially unreliable judgements by the data collector or recorder. As a result they are inevitably crude and mechanical in their operation and take very inadequate account of variation in the allocation of economic and social roles within households.

The rules actually used in official statistical applications owe much to the precedents provided by successive Censuses of Population. In the UK, censuses have never attempted to collect information on individual income or earnings or to enquire directly into households' financial arrangements. Hence a direct approach to identifying a 'chief economic supporter' has been ruled out. On the other hand the concept of the 'householder' as a person who represents the household (and can be held responsible for seeing that the census form is filled in) is built into census practice. Hence it is a version of the 'householder' or 'head of household' concept which has historically been developed on censuses to fill the reference person role. This precedent has been followed by many household surveys, though often with some refinements.

The rules used to identify a household reference person have therefore been broadly as follows. In one- or two-generation family households the oldest adult male is generally taken to be the reference person for allocating socio-economic status. In the always significant minority of households containing no eligible males a female must obviously be selected, again usually on criteria of seniority.

However, modifications to this rule are often introduced in survey practice, particularly to deal with households containing several adults who are unrelated or of different generations. For example, seniority and/or gender may be overruled in order to give preference to an economically active over an inactive person, or to the person in whose name the living accommodation is owned or rented. These modifications may be viewed partly as attempts to get closer to the 'chief economic supporter' concept without having to ask about income.

Adopting a single individual chosen in this way as household reference person has been seen as the best available solution in the context of standardised data collection, since it has the great practical advantages of using only mechanical selection rules and of simplifying the process of allocating socio-economic status in problematic cases.

7.4.1 Problems in the use of household reference persons and possible alternative strategies

The single reference person approach has always produced anomalies in particular cases; and social and economic trends over recent decades have caused the validity of assigning socio-economic status to households and their members in this way increasingly to be challenged. The technical issues have been somewhat overshadowed by objections to the patriarchal and authoritarian overtones of the term 'head of household', when combined with the deliberate male bias of the selection rules. The term 'head of household' is gradually falling out of use, but the problems which give rise to the need to define a 'household reference person' remain.

The two essential issues which have to be faced are:

- Is it essential to use occupation-referenced methods to assign socio-economic status to households and their members?

- If so, to whose occupation(s) should reference be made?

As regards the first issue, other possible indicators of socio-economic status may be proposed, such as income, assets, housing tenure, educational or vocational qualifications, etc. On closer examination the use of such indicators often raises technical problems at least as severe as does the use of occupation. In some cases the required information is not readily available from censuses or other standard sources in this country; in others the available data do not yield a sensitive and consistent indicator; and in others again the relationship between the alternative indicator and socio-economic status is thought to be more shifting and fallible than the relationship between occupation and socio-economic status. Occupation-derived measures are relatively sensitive, readily available, and closely related to position in society. Also, of course, there is a powerful weight of precedent supporting the use of occupation-referencing methods.

It has nevertheless been shown that a composite census-derived measure applicable at the household level, based on whether or not a household has access to car or van and on its housing tenure, accounts for rather more of the variance in standardised mortality ratios than does Social Class based on Occupation (though still more variance is accounted for when both are used together). It is likely that household-level measures of this type have comparable explanatory power in other fields of social analysis.

An objection to relying on such measures is that their validity depends upon the distribution of certain household attributes over a limited historical period; in the nineteen twenties and thirties the indices would have needed to be different from those found best in the seventies and eighties, and they will no doubt have to change again in future. However, as argued above at Section 7.1, the way in which occupation is related to socio-economic status also changes over time and this needs to be reflected by changing the referencing conventions. In thinking of occupation as a durable indicator we must consider not only cases such as barristers, who were a clearly-defined sub-group in Social Class I in 1911 and remain so in 1990, but also cases such as computer programmers, who scarcely existed before the nineteen sixties and whose position in the employment and socio-economic structures has certainly been changing continuously since then.

The conclusion to be drawn here is that occupation-based measures and household-level measures such as that described can both make useful and distinguishable contributions to the explanation of socio-demographic phenomena. The contributions overlap, however; and in practical situations the robustness and simplicity, from both data-collection and data-processing viewpoints, of the household-level measures is attractive, when compared with the technical and conceptual difficulties of deriving socio-economic status from occupation.

The second issue concerns how to select household reference person(s) for socio-economic classification. The validity of identifying a single reference person, and of doing so according to rules which select husbands and senior males rather than wives or senior females, has certainly been eroded. One reason has been the rising prevalence in recent decades of multi-earner households whose standard of living (clearly) and socio-economic status (arguably) is heavily influenced by the presence of several, rather than just one, substantial 'economic supporters'. Another has been wider acceptance of the view that the educational and social attributes of adult females in households or families affect those of the household as a whole at least as much as those of their partners.

Conceptually the ideal would be to move to some method of assigning socio-economic status to the household which would take account of the attributes of one or several persons, as appropriate, and would be analogous to calculating 'total household income', as opposed to taking the income of the household reference person. Perhaps, too, the group to which the occupation-derived socio-economic status of reference person(s) is ascribed should not be the household as conventionally defined, but some grouping thought to be more tightly-knit in social and economic terms, such as the family unit or the 'minimal household unit'.

All large-scale practical applications such as censuses have an overarching requirement for simple, robust, economical, and readily reproducible methods. In the judgement of OPCS and other producers of statistics no method of choosing multiple reference persons, or of combining occupational information for several persons to determine socio-economic status, has so far been proposed which meets these criteria. Aside from practical constraints, methods which are less valid for their purpose, or which introduce more inconsistencies and arbitrary assumptions, than the present generally-used method of identifying a single reference person should be avoided.

In an effort to escape from this dilemma it has been argued that the present, single reference person, method should at least be modified to remove the present built-in bias in favour of selecting males. One way of doing that in households containing several employed adults would be to capture the occupations (and also the employment and full-time/part-time statuses) of all the persons concerned, to compare them and to classify the household and its members by reference to the 'dominant' occupation (e.g. the highest-status full-time occupation).

Even if one accepts the method of determining which occupation is 'dominant', such an approach would in many applications significantly increase the burden and cost of collecting, coding, and processing occupational information. Moreover, the overall effect would be relatively small, since it can be shown that in the majority of cases the 'dominant' occupation would be that of the person selected as reference person by current methods, or one equivalent to it in socio-economic terms. There are, of course, instances where a female spouse has an occupation which would be judged 'dominant' over that of her partner (the reference person on current rules) but they are relatively rare.

In general, it is amply clear from survey and other evidence that taking the occupation of a senior adult male, while admittedly highly fallible, on average gives a much better indicator of the socio-economic position of the household than would taking that of an adult female (or other adult household member).

8. Compatibility between SOC and ISCO 88

The International Standard Classification of Occupations (ISCO) has been developed starting earlier this century by the International Labour Organisation (ILO). Some countries which did not already have well-developed national systems of their own adopted the 1968 version of ISCO as their national standard.

In the mid-nineteen eighties an ILO technical team set about revising ISCO 68, to produce a new version to be known as ISCO 88. This will come into general use in 1990-91. Some countries will again adopt it as their standard. Others, including the UK, France, and West Germany, will retain their own classifications, which have been developed with their particular national needs in mind.

ISCO 88 is the basis of several initiatives intended to improve international comparability of information on occupations. The UK and other countries have agreed to provide information on occupations from the 1990-91 round of population censuses which conforms to ISCO 88 or some best fit to it. The Statistical Office of the European Community has undertaken a project to define a standard classificatory framework for occupations, starting from ISCO 88, for use within the EC. This project is proceeding through consultation with the statistical offices of the individual EC countries. Countries retaining their own classifications will agree conventions for harmonising their own classifications with an EC standard for purposes of making statistical comparisons within the Community. For the UK this raises the issue of how best to assimilate SOC to an ISCO-derived framework.

There is in fact a close similarity between SOC and ISCO 88 in terms of the principles of classification adopted, type of structure, and level of detail aimed at. The parallel development of ISCO 88 by the ILO team was taken into account in the development of SOC. This mainly affected decisions on how the 371 SOC OUGs should be allocated at higher levels of the SOC structure. In practice issues raised by group definition at higher and lower levels of detail tend to interact, so some adjustments at the lower levels of SOC were also made to achieve better compatibility with ISCO 88.

In many areas the correspondence between SOC and ISCO 88 is good down to Unit Group level. However, there are also several important areas where it is harder to achieve meaningful harmonisation. These affect higher as well as lower levels of the two classifications. In general it is these areas which have presented difficulty for other countries as well and they tend to reflect limitations of the raw data available, as well as some differences in conceptual approach. It is nevertheless expected that an acceptable harmonisation will be achieved between SOC and the European Community implementation of ISCO 88.

9. Arrangements for introducing SOC in official applications

9.1 The 1991 Census of Population in Great Britain

As in previous GB censuses, occupational information on a 10% systematic sample of census forms only will be coded in the 1991 Census. To assist census users who wish to continue up to 1991 historical series of occupational statistics based on CO80, a specially developed frame will be used for census occupational coding which includes all the distinctions between occupational groups made in CO80 and also all those made in SOC. This will enable results to be produced on the basis either of CO80 or of SOC.

It is planned to produce a considerable amount of statistical output, mainly in the form of tables at both national and local (small area) level, in which occupational and socio-economic classifications will feature. The classificatory basis for almost all the published census results using occupation will be SOC for occupation as such and the SOC-based versions of the socio-economic classifications. For occupation, detail down to Unit Group level will be provided in national tables, while at small area level results will be at the two most aggregated levels of classification in SOC (Major and Sub-major Groups).

Only a very limited amount of published output will be based on CO80, but some additional tables based on CO80 may be run and made available on request and it will be possible to order special tables on repayment. No results will be produced based on the composite occupational coding frame, since the component groups distinguished have no significance in their own right.

In addition to occupation, information on status in employment, higher qualifications, and name and address of employing establishment will be obtained from census households and captured for the 10% sample. Information on industry and number of other employees will be linked in to the census database by reference to the 1989 Census of Employment. In census coding practice some use will be made of industry and higher qualifications codes in classifying occupations otherwise inadequately specified (see Section 3 above).

The coding of occupations in the census will be carried out using a computer-assisted system based on SOC. It is expected that this will be more economical and lead to more reliable coding, but the results will be consistent with those of SOC coding done clerically using the SOC Volumes.

A new source for users wishing to carry out further analysis of census data at the level of households or individuals will be the samples of anonymised records (SARs) from the 1991 Census which it is planned to make available in 1992. It is expected that full SOC occupational detail will be available in the SAR files.

9.2 Other major official sources of statistical information on occupation

It is planned to introduce SOC coding during 1990-91 to other major governmental sources of statistical information on occupations. The main recurrent sources affected at the level of detailed occupational coding will be the Labour Force Survey and the New Earnings Survey.

For the Annual and Quarterly Labour Force Surveys it is planned to use during 1991 the special composite coding frame developed for the 1991 Census (see Section 9.1) and then to move to SOC. This will allow users to link the 1991 results either to the series produced during the nineteen eighties, using the pre-SOC versions of Condensed KOS etc., or to the SOC-based series which will be built up over the nineteen nineties.

On the New Earnings Survey (NES), SOC will be introduced with the presentation of the 1991 results. Additionally, the 1990 occupational information has been recoded to SOC at the Unit Group level as well as being coded to the previous KOS system; and it is intended to publish selected results of the 1990 survey using SOC at the same time as the results of the 1991 survey are published. While it is expected that the standard NES analyses by occupation will be produced from 1991 onwards at the SOC Unit Group level, certain additional cross-analyses, for example of occupation within region or within industry, are more likely to be published at the Minor Group level, or possibly even at the Sub-major or even Major Group level, depending upon the size of the subsample and the reliability of the the resulting estimates of average earnings.

Hitherto the NES has used uncondensed KOS for classifying occupations. The results of the dual coding of 1990 data should be a useful tool in interpreting the effects of the change-over to SOC and may provide a usable link for translating pre-1990 KOS-based NES results onto a SOC basis. The effectiveness of such a link has not yet been established, but a considerable number of discontinuities can be expected.

In the Employment Department SOC has been in use for managing information on Employment Training and Youth Training since April 1990. Training and Enterprise Councils (TECs) are being provided with local labour market information gathering systems which use SOC for all occupational information. NOMIS, the Employment Department's nationally networked information system, will include occupational information classified by SOC as it becomes available (e.g. from the 1991 Census of Population). Mappings between SOC and existing occupational classifications will be utilised on the system to permit comparability between new, SOC-based information and historical data as far as possible.

9.3 Official client-oriented applications

The Employment Service will introduce SOC into all its local offices towards the end of 1991 to classify vacancies held and the occupations of clients claiming benefits. The Employment Service carries out periodic surveys of claimant characteristics using information recorded on administrative forms, and from 1991 these will use SOC instead of CODOT as at present.

Selected references

Britton M and Birch F (1985). *1981 Census Post Enumeration Survey*, HMSO.

Department of Employment (1972). *Classification of Occupations and Directory of Occupational Titles*, HMSO.

Goldthorpe J H and Hope K (1974). *The Social Grading of Occupations: A New Approach and Scale*, Oxford, Clarendon Press.

International Labour Office (1990). *International Standard Classification of Occupations 1988*, ILO.

Monk D (1985). *Social Grading on the National Readership Survey*, London: Joint Industry Committee for National Readership Surveys.

Office of Population Censuses and Surveys (1980). *Classification of Occupations 1980*, HMSO.

Office of Population and Censuses and Surveys; and Employment Department Group (1990). *Standard Occupational Classification, Volume 1: Structure of the Classification*, HMSO.

Office of Population and Censuses and Surveys; and Employment Department Group (1990). *Standard Occupational Classification , Volume 2: Coding Index*, HMSO.

Stevenson T H C (1928). The vital statistics of wealth and poverty, *Journal of the Royal Statistical Society*, 91.

Thomas R and Elias P (1989). Development of the Standard Occupational Classification, *Population Trends*, 55.

	No. of OPCS operational occupation codes	%	No. of economically active persons (10%)	%
SECTION 1				
a) Comparability not possible by combining C080 operational codes	94	26.8	770,530	33.5
b) A measure of comparability possible by combining whole C080 operational codes*	42	12.0	112,773	4.9
c) Combination of a + b	136	38.8	883,303	38.4
SECTION 2				
Directly comparable	197	56.3	1,058,512	46.0
SECTION 3				
Comparability possible by aggregation	17	4.9	358,609	15.6
TOTAL	**350**	**100.0**	**2,300,424**	**100.0**

*15 combinations of two C080 operational codes.
  2 combinations of three C080 operational codes.
  1 combination of six C080 operational codes.

Condensed KOS code	Condensed KOS group heading	% difference rebased
001	Judges, barristers, advocates, solicitors	.00
002	Accountants, valuers, finance specialists	.00
003	Personnel and industrial relations managers; O and M, work study and operational research officers	4.59
004	Economists, statisticians, systems analysts, computer programmers	-.60
005	Marketing, sales, advertising, public relations and purchasing managers	.00
006	Statutory and other inspectors	-2.28
007	General administrators - national government	.00
008	Local government officers (administrative and executive functions)	9.36
009	All other professional and related supporting management and administration	-6.75
010	Teachers in higher education	.00
011	Teachers n.e.c.	.85
012	Vocational and industrial trainers, education officers, social and behavioural scientists	-5.23
013	Welfare workers	-1.81
014	Clergy, ministers of religion	.00
015	Medical and dental practitioners	.00
016	Nurse administrators, nurses	1.43
017	Pharmacists, radiographers, therapists n.e.c.	1.14
018	All other professional and related in education, welfare and health	-6.52
019	Authors, writers, journalists	.00
020	Artists, designers, window dressers	-4.35
021	Actors, musicians, entertainers, stage managers	.00
022	Photographers, cameramen, sound and vision equipment operators	.00
023	All other literary, artistic and sports	7.25
024	Scientists, physicists, mathematicians	-.21
025	Civil, structural, municipal, mining and quarrying engineers	.00
026	Mechanical and aeronautical engineers	9.79
027	Electrical and electronic engineers	-11.90
028	Engineers and technologists n.e.c.	-9.18
029	Draughtsmen	-8.50
030	Laboratory and engineering technicians, technician engineers	.00
031	Architects, town planners, quantity, building and land surveyors	.00
032	Officers (ships and aircraft), air traffic planners and controllers	.51
033	Professional and related in science, engineering and other technologies and similar fields n.e.c.	2.76
034	Production, works and maintenance managers, works foremen	10.66
035	Site and other managers, agents and clerks of works, general foremen (building and civil engineering)	-7.10
036	Managers in transport, warehousing, public utilities and mining	-4.11
037	Office managers	-1.27
038	Managers in wholesale and retail distribution	1.13
039	Managers of hotels, clubs, etc., and in entertainment and sport	3.72

Table 2 - *continued*

Condensed KOS code	Condensed KOS group heading	% difference rebased
040	Farmers, horticulturists, farm managers	.00
041	Officers, UK armed forces	.00
042	Officers, foreign and Commonwealth armed forces	.00
043	Senior police, prison and fire service officers	.00
044	All other managers	-11.94
045	Supervisors of clerks, civil service executive officers	-65.80
046	Clerks	5.02
047	Retail shop cashiers, check-out and cash wrap operators	4.43
048	Supervisors of typists, office machine operators, telephonists, etc.	-100.00
049	Secretaries, shorthand typists, receptionists	1.32
050	Office machine operators	9.21
051	Telephonists, radio and telegraph operators	8.51
052	Supervisors of postmen, mail sorters, messengers	-100.00
053	Postmen, mail sorters, messengers	5.30
054	Sales supervisors	-100.00
055	Salesmen, sales assistants, shop assistants, shelf fillers, petrol pump, forecourt attendants	3.63
056	Roundsmen, van salesmen	6.44
057	Sales representatives and agents	-.24
058	NCOs and other ranks, UK armed forces	.00
059	NCOs and other ranks, foreign and Commonwealth armed forces	.00
060	Supervisors (police sergeants, fire fighting and related)	-100.00
061	Policemen, firemen, prison officers	11.29
062	Other security and protective service workers	5.97
063	Catering supervisors	-100.00
064	Chefs, cooks	13.56
065	Waiters and bar staff	5.26
066	Counter hands, assistants, kitchen porters, hands	3.61
067	Supervisors - housekeeping and related	-82.24
068	Domestic staff and school helpers	-62.57
069	Travel stewards and attendants, hospital and hotel porters	2.26
070	Ambulancemen, hospital orderlies	-3.66
071	Supervisors, foremen - caretaking, cleaning and related	-100.00
072	Caretakers, road sweepers and other cleaners	53.32
073	Hairdressing supervisors	-100.00
074	Hairdressers, barbers	.49
075	All other in catering, cleaning and other personal service	-2.50
076	Foremen - farming, horticulture, forestry	-100.00
077	Farm workers	3.99
078	Horticultural workers, gardeners, groundsmen	7.28
079	Agricultural machinery drivers, operators	1.34
080	Forestry workers	22.07

Table 2 - *continued*

Condensed KOS code	Condensed KOS group heading	% difference rebased
081	Supervisors, mates - fishing	-100.00
082	Fishermen	1.52
083	All other in farming and related	2.96
084	Foremen - tannery and leather (including leather substitutes) working	-100.00
085	Tannery and leather (including leather substitutes) workers	25.56
086	Foremen - textile processing	-100.00
087	Textile workers	.45
088	Foremen - chemical processing	-100.00
089	Chemical, gas and petroleum process plant operators	23.21
090	Foremen - food and drink processing	-100.00
091	Bakers, flour confectioners	14.91
092	Butchers	2.25
093	Foremen - paper and board making and paper products	-100.00
094	Paper, board and paper product makers, bookbinders	-40.86
095	Foremen - glass, ceramics, rubber, plastics, etc.	-100.00
096	Glass and ceramics furnacemen and workers	19.17
097	Rubber and plastics workers	-100.00
098	All other in processing materials (other than metal)	16.37
099	Foremen - printing	-100.00
100	Printing workers, screen and block printers	6.19
101	Foremen - textile materials working	-100.00
102	Tailors, dressmakers and other clothing workers	6.09
103	Coach trimmers, upholsterers, mattress makers	3.41
104	Foremen - woodworking	-100.00
105	Woodworkers, pattern makers	5.34
106	Sawyers, veneer cutters, woodworking machinists	5.10
107	All other in making and repairing (excluding metal and electrical)	16.37
108	Foremen - metal making and treating	-100.00
109	Furnacemen (metal), rollermen, smiths, forgemen	8.33
110	Metal drawers, moulders, die casters, electroplaters, annealers	25.25
111	Foremen - engineering machining	-100.00
112	Press and machine tool setter operators and operators, turners	4.33
113	Machine attendants, minders, press and stamping machine operators, metal polishers, fettlers, dressers	3.37
114	Foremen - production fitting (metal)	-100.00
115	Tool makers, tool fitters, markers-out	8.94
116	Instrument and watch and clock makers and repairers	10.30
117	Metal working production fitters and fitter/machinists	7.05
118	Motor vehicle and aircraft mechanics	5.10
119	Office machinery mechanics	3.22
120	Foremen - production fitting and wiring (electrical)	-100.00

Table 2 - *continued*

Condensed KOS code	Condensed KOS group heading	% difference rebased
121	Production fitters, electricians, electricity power plant operators, switchboard attendants	13.98
122	Telephone fitters, cable jointers, linesmen	5.47
123	Radio, TV and other electronic maintenance fitters and mechanics	3.52
124	Foremen - metal working, pipes, sheets, structures	-100.00
125	Plumbers, heating and ventilating fitters, gas fitters	5.20
126	Sheet metal workers, platers, shipwrights, riveters, etc.	4.73
127	Steel erectors, scaffolders, steel benders, fixers	39.19
128	Welders	3.25
129	Foremen - other processing, making and repairing (metal and electrical)	-100.00
130	Goldsmiths, silversmiths, etc., engravers, etchers	-22.37
131	All other in processing, making and repairing (metal and electrical)	-6.60
132	Foremen - painting and similar coating	-100.00
133	Painters, decorators, french polishers	.31
134	Foremen - product assembling (repetitive)	-100.00
135	Repetitive assemblers (metal and electrical goods)	20.14
136	Foremen - product inspection and packaging	-100.00
137	Inspectors, viewers, testers, packers, bottlers, etc.	4.52
138	All other in painting, repetitive assembling, product inspection, packaging and related	5.94
139	Foremen - building and civil engineering n.e.c.	-100.00
140	Building and construction workers	-2.84
141	Concreters, road surfacers, railway lengthmen	17.25
142	Sewage plant attendants, sewermen (maintenance), mains and service layers, pipe jointers (gas, water, drainage, oil), inspectors (water supply), turncocks	30.42
143	Civil engineering labourers, craftsmen's mates and other builders' labourers n.e.c.	4.88
144	Foremen/deputies - coalmining	-100.00
145	Face-trained coalmining workers	23.00
146	All other in construction, mining, quarrying, well drilling and related n.e.c.	55.75
147	Foremen - ships, lighters and other vessels	-100.00
148	Deck, engine-room hands, bargemen, lightermen, boatmen	5.82
149	Foremen - rail transport operating	-100.00
150	Rail transport operating staff	14.96
151	Foremen - road transport operating, bus inspectors	-25.88
152	Bus, coach, lorry drivers, etc.	.23
153	Bus conductors, drivers' mates	.00
154	Foremen - civil engineering plant operating, materials handling equipment operating	-100.00
155	Mechanical plant, fork lift, mechanical truck drivers, crane drivers, operators	1.27
156	Foremen - materials moving and storing	-100.00
157	Storekeepers, stevedores, warehouse, market and other goods porters	12.89
158	All other in transport operating, materials moving and storing and related n.e.c.	.20
159	Foremen - miscellaneous	-100.00
160	General labourers	1.56
161	All other in miscellaneous occupations n.e.c.	-62.63

Where rebased difference shows 100% change, Condensed KOS were previously Foremen/Supervisor status with the exception of code 097 - Rubber and plastics workers.

Table 3 Comparison of Social Class allocations between C080 and SOC

1981 Census
England and Wales economically active persons 10%

| | 1980 Social Class | | | | | | | | | |
	I	II	IIIN	IIIM	IV	V	Armed forces and inadequately described	Total	%	% difference
I	**85,012**	1,743	-	-	-	-	-	86,755	3.8	-
II	1,575	**483,859**	3,387	7	929	-	-	489,757	21.3	+0.2
Social IIIN	-	493	**502,661**	-	275	-	-	503,429	21.9	-0.1
Class IIIM	-	36	-	**548,080**	1,302	-	-	549,418	23.9	-0.3
altered IV	-	-	279	8,328	**377,197**	-	-	385,804	16.8	-1.2
by V	-	-	-	212	33,312	**142,799**	-	176,323	7.6	+1.4
SOC Armed forces and inadequately described	-	-	-	-	-	-	**108,938**	108,938	4.7	-
TOTAL	86,587	486,131	506,327	556,627	413,015	142,799	108,938	2,300,424	100	-
%	3.8	21.1	22.0	24.2	18.0	6.2	4.7		100	

Table 4 Comparison of Socio-economic Group allocations between C080 and SOC

1981 Census

England and Wales economically active persons 10%

1980 Socio-economic Groups (SEG)	1.1, 2.1	1.2, 2.2	3	4	5.1	5.2	6	7	8	9	10	11	12	13	14	15	16	17	Total	%	% difference
1.1, 2.1	**45,891**	-	-	-	80	-	-	-	-	-	-	-	-	-	-	-	-	-	45,971	2.0	-
1.2, 2.2	-	**213,552**	37	1,262	2,107	-	-	-	-	-	-	-	-	-	-	-	-	-	216,958	9.4	-
3	16	-	**14,292**	-	73	-	-	-	-	-	-	-	-	-	-	-	-	-	14,381	0.6	-
4	-	73	-	**70,465**	1,577	-	-	-	-	-	-	-	-	-	-	-	-	-	72,115	3.1	-
5.1	-	2,721	111	165	**204,970**	53	696	-	-	-	758	-	56	-	-	-	-	-	209,530	9.1	-
5.2	-	-	-	-	-	**22,068**	-	-	-	-	-	-	-	-	-	-	-	-	22,068	1.0	-
6 (SEG	-	-	-	-	467	-	**468,882**	-	-	-	-	-	-	-	-	-	-	-	469,329	20.4	-
7	-	3	-	-	-	-	-	**91,062**	36	-	868	-	140	-	-	-	-	-	92,109	4.0	-1.4
8 (altered	-	45	-	-	-	-	-	600	**56,243**	-	-	-	-	-	-	-	-	-	56,888	2.5	-
9	-	-	-	-	-	-	-	-	-	**396,594**	1,040	-	-	-	-	-	-	-	397,634	17.3	-0.2
10 (by	56	11	-	-	-	-	214	-	110	5,388	**279,917**	-	87	-	-	-	-	-	285,783	12.5	+0.2
11	-	-	-	-	-	-	-	31,592	-	-	1,230	**138,713**	99	-	-	-	-	-	171,634	7.5	+1.5
12 (SOC	12	-	-	-	24	-	-	-	-	-	-	-	**95,226**	-	-	-	-	-	95,262	4.1	-0.1
13	-	-	-	-	-	-	-	-	-	-	-	-	-	**10,224**	-	-	-	-	10,224	0.4	-
14	-	-	-	-	-	-	-	-	-	-	-	-	-	-	**10,377**	-	-	-	10,377	0.5	-
15	-	-	-	-	-	-	-	-	-	-	-	-	-	-	-	**21,223**	-	-	21,223	0.9	-
16	-	-	-	-	-	-	-	-	-	-	-	-	-	-	-	-	**23,893**	-	23,893	1.0	-
17	-	-	-	-	-	-	-	-	-	-	-	-	-	-	-	-	-	**85,045**	85,045	3.7	-
Total	45,975	216,405	14,440	71,892	209,298	22,121	469,772	123,254	56,389	401,982	283,813	138,713	95,608	10,224	10,377	21,223	23,893	85,045	2,300,424		
%	2.0	9.4	0.6	3.1	9.1	1.0	20.4	5.4	2.5	17.5	12.3	6.0	4.2	0.4	0.5	0.9	1.0	3.7	-		

(Side annotation spanning rows 6–12: "SEG altered by SOC")

35

APPENDICES

Appendix A. Allocation of SOC Occupational Unit Groups to Social Classes and Socio-economic Groups

Table A1 shows in tabular form the allocation of SOC Occupational Unit Groups to Social Classes and Socio-economic Groups, using the maximum-continuity principle (see Section 6.1). The table also shows how other information, on Status in Employment (specifically, whether the person has Self-employed or Supervisory status) and on whether or not self-employed persons have employees, is used to help determine the socio-economic allocation of certain OUGs. Table A1 thus provides for SOC the same information that the table given at Appendix B of the Classification of Occupations 1980 gave for CO80.

To use the table to determine the Social Class or SEG code(s) corresponding to a SOC Occupational Unit Group, consult the row corresponding to the SOC OUG concerned. Then find the appropriate column defined by Status in Employment etc. and read off from the cell where row and column intersect the relevant SC (Roman numeral) or SEG (Arabic numeral) coding.

Like its predecessor, Table A1 contains numerous blank cells. These correspond to situations deemed not to arise, such as a self-employed railway guard, for example. In practice some responses made by the public correspond to blank (non-permissible) cells, and in census practice these cases are edited by changing either the OUG or the Status in Employment coding so as to achieve a permissible combination. This editing has the effect of correcting some miscoded or miskeyed responses, but it can be argued that the conventions used do not take account of all possible situations which may actually occur under changing circumstances and new legal adjudications in the real world. This may happen for example, where a person is recorded as self-employed, and at least in some legal senses is so, but is in an occupation where self-employment is deemed under the editing conventions not to occur.

Another census coding convention implicit in Table A1 is that members of the Armed Forces are not assigned to a substantive Social Class. This is because of limitations on the occupational information collected about such persons in censuses. A special Socio-economic Group is assigned to Members of the Armed Forces.

Table A1 SOC - Derivation of Social Class and Socio-economic Groups

Standard occupational classification unit groups within minor groups	Manual Non-manual	Self-employed with employees S.E.G.	Social Class	Self-employed without employees S.E.G.	Social Class	Managers S.E.G.	Social Class	Foremen S.E.G.	Social Class	Apprentices, etc., Employees n.e.c. S.E.G.	Social Class
10 GENERAL MANAGERS AND ADMINISTRATORS IN NATIONAL AND LOCAL GOVERNMENT, LARGE COMPANIES AND ORGANISATIONS											
100 General administrators; national government (Assistant Secretary/Grade 5 and above)	NM	-	-	-	-	1.2	I	-	-	-	-
101 General managers; large companies and organisations	NM	-	-	-	-	1.2	II	-	-	-	-
102 Local government officers (administrative and executive functions)	NM	-	-	-	-	1.2	II	-	-	-	-
103 General administrators; national government (HEO to Senior Principal/Grade 6)	NM	-	-	-	-	1.2	II	-	-	-	-
11 PRODUCTION MANAGERS IN MANUFACTURING, CONSTRUCTION, MINING AND ENERGY INDUSTRIES											
110 Production, works and maintenance managers	NM	-	-	-	-	1.2, 2.2	II	5.2	IIIN	-	-
111 Managers in building and contracting	NM	-	-	-	-	1.2, 2.2	II	-	-	-	-
112 Clerks of works	NM	-	-	-	-	-	-	-	-	6	IIIN
113 Managers in mining and energy industries	NM	-	-	-	-	1.2, 2.2	II	-	-	-	-
12 SPECIALIST MANAGERS											
120 Treasurers and company financial managers	NM	-	-	-	-	1.2, 2.2	II	-	-	-	-
121 Marketing and sales managers	NM	1.1, 2.1	II	5.1	II	1.2, 2.2	II	-	-	-	-
122 Purchasing managers	NM	-	-	-	-	1.2, 2.2	II	-	-	-	-
123 Advertising and public relations managers	NM	1.1, 2.1	II	5.1	II	1.2, 2.2	II	-	-	-	-
124 Personnel, training and industrial relations managers	NM	-	-	-	-	1.2, 2.2	II	-	-	-	-
125 Organisation and methods and work study managers	NM	-	-	-	-	1.2, 2.2	II	-	-	-	-
126 Computer systems and data processing managers	NM	-	-	-	-	1.2, 2.2	II	-	-	-	-
127 Company secretaries	NM	5.1	II	5.1	II	1.2, 2.2	II	-	-	-	-
13 FINANCIAL INSTITUTION AND OFFICE MANAGERS, CIVIL SERVICE EXECUTIVE OFFICERS											
130 Credit controllers	NM	-	-	-	-	1.2, 2.2	II	-	-	-	-
131 Bank, Building Society and Post Office managers (except self-employed)	NM	-	-	-	-	1.2, 2.2	II	-	-	-	-
132 Civil Service executive officers	NM	-	-	-	-	-	-	5.1	II	-	-
139 Other financial institution and office managers n.e.c.	NM	1.1, 2.1	II	12	II	1.2, 2.2	II	-	-	-	-
14 MANAGERS IN TRANSPORT AND STORING											
140 Transport managers	NM	-	-	-	-	1.2, 2.2	II	-	-	-	-
141 Stores controllers	NM	-	-	-	-	1.2, 2.2	II	-	-	-	-
142 Managers in warehousing and other materials handling	NM	-	-	-	-	1.2, 2.2	II	-	-	-	-

Table A1 - *continued*

Standard occupational classification unit groups within minor groups	Manual Non-manual	Self-employed with employees S.E.G.	Self-employed with employees Social Class	Self-employed without employees S.E.G.	Self-employed without employees Social Class	Managers S.E.G.	Managers Social Class	Foremen S.E.G.	Foremen Social Class	Apprentices, etc., Employees n.e.c. S.E.G.	Apprentices, etc., Employees n.e.c. Social Class
15 PROTECTIVE SERVICE OFFICERS											
150 Officers in UK armed forces	-	-	-	-	-	16	-	-	-	-	-
151 Officers in foreign and Commonwealth armed forces	-	-	-	-	-	16	-	-	-	-	-
152 Police officers (inspector and above)	NM	-	-	-	-	1.2	II	-	-	-	-
153 Fire service officers (station officer and above)	NM	-	-	-	-	1.2	II	-	-	-	-
154 Prison officers (principal officer and above)	NM	-	-	-	-	1.2	II	-	-	-	-
155 Customs and excise, immigration service officers (customs: chief preventive officer and above; excise: surveyor and above)	NM	-	-	-	-	-	-	-	-	5.1	II
16 MANAGERS IN FARMING, HORTICULTURE, FORESTRY AND FISHING											
160 Farm owners and managers, horticulturists	NM	13	II	14	II	13	II	-	-	-	-
169 Other managers in farming, horticulture, forestry and fishing n.e.c.	NM	1.1, 2.1	II	12	II	1.2, 2.2	II	-	-	-	-
17 MANAGERS AND PROPRIETORS IN SERVICE INDUSTRIES											
170 Property and estate managers	NM	5.1	II	5.1	II	1.2, 2.2	II	-	-	-	-
171 Garage managers and proprietors	NM	1.1, 2.1	II	12	II	1.2, 2.2	II	-	-	-	-
172 Hairdressers' and barbers' managers and proprietors	NM	1.1, 2.1	IIIN	12	IIIN	1.2, 2.2	II	-	-	-	-
173 Hotel and accommodation managers	NM	1.1, 2.1	II	12	II	1.2, 2.2	II	-	-	-	-
174 Restaurant and catering managers	NM	1.1, 2.1	IIIN	12	IIIN	1.2, 2.2	II	-	-	-	-
175 Publicans, innkeepers and club stewards	NM	1.1, 2.1	II	12	II	1.2, 2.2	II	-	-	-	-
176 Entertainment and sports managers	NM	1.1, 2.1	IIIN	12	IIIN	1.2, 2.2	II	-	-	-	-
177 Travel agency managers	NM	1.1, 2.1	II	12	II	1.2, 2.2	II	-	-	-	-
178 Managers and proprietors of butchers and fishmongers	NM	1.1, 2.1	IIIN	12	IIIN	1.2, 2.2	II	-	-	-	-
179 Managers and proprietors in service industries n.e.c.	NM	1.1, 2.1	II	12	II	1.2, 2.2	II	-	-	-	-
19 MANAGERS AND ADMINISTRATORS NEC											
190 Officials of trade associations, trade unions, professional bodies and charities	NM	-	-	-	-	1.2, 2.2	II	-	-	5.1	II
191 Registrars and administrators of educational establishments	NM	-	-	-	-	1.2, 2.2	II	-	-	-	-
199 Other managers and administrators n.e.c.	NM	1.1, 2.1	II	12	II	1.2, 2.2	II	-	-	-	-
20 NATURAL SCIENTISTS											
200 Chemists	NM	3	I	3	I	-	-	-	-	4	I
201 Biological scientists and biochemists	NM	3	I	3	I	-	-	-	-	4	I

Standard occupational classification unit groups within minor groups	Manual Non-manual	EMPLOYMENT STATUS									
		Self-employed				Managers		Foremen		Apprentices, etc., Employees n.e.c.	
		with employees		without employees							
		S.E.G.	Social Class	S.E.G.	Social Class	S.E.G.	Social Class	S.E.G.	Social Class	S.E.G.	Social Class
202 Physicists, geologists and meteorologists	NM	3	I	3	I	-	-	-	-	4	I
209 Other natural scientists n.e.c.	NM	3	I	3	I	-	-	-	-	4	I
21 ENGINEERS AND TECHNOLOGISTS											
210 Civil, structural, municipal, mining and quarrying engineers	NM	3	I	3	I	-	-	-	-	4	I
211 Mechanical engineers	NM	3	I	3	I	-	-	-	-	4	I
212 Electrical engineers	NM	3	I	3	I	-	-	-	-	4	I
213 Electronic engineers	NM	3	I	3	I	-	-	-	-	4	I
214 Software engineers	NM	3	I	3	I	-	-	-	-	4	I
215 Chemical engineers	NM	3	I	3	I	-	-	-	-	4	I
216 Design and development engineers	NM	3	I	3	I	-	-	-	-	4	I
217 Process and production engineers	NM	3	I	3	I	-	-	-	-	4	I
218 Planning and quality control engineers	NM	3	I	3	I	-	-	-	-	4	I
219 Other engineers and technologists n.e.c.	NM	3	I	3	I	-	-	-	-	4	I
22 HEALTH PROFESSIONALS											
220 Medical practitioners	NM	3	I	3	I	-	-	-	-	4	I
221 Pharmacists/pharmacologists	NM	3	I	3	I	-	-	-	-	4	I
222 Ophthalmic opticians	NM	3	I	3	I	-	-	-	-	4	I
223 Dental practitioners	NM	3	I	3	I	-	-	-	-	4	I
224 Veterinarians	NM	3	I	3	I	-	-	-	-	4	I
23 TEACHING PROFESSIONALS											
230 University and polytechnic teaching professionals	NM	3	I	3	I	-	-	-	-	4	I
231 Higher and further education teaching professionals	NM	5.1	II	5.1	II	1.2, 2.2	II	-	-	5.1	II
232 Education officers, school inspectors	NM	-	-	-	-	-	-	-	-	4	I
233 Secondary (and middle school deemed secondary) education teaching professionals	NM	5.1	II	5.1	II	1.2, 2.2	II	-	-	5.1	II
234 Primary (and middle school deemed primary) and nursery education teaching professionals	NM	5.1	II	5.1	II	1.2, 2.2	II	-	-	5.1	II
235 Special education teaching professionals	NM	5.1	II	5.1	II	1.2, 2.2	II	-	-	5.1	II
239 Other teaching professionals n.e.c.	NM	5.1	II	5.1	II	1.2, 2.2	II	-	-	5.1	II
24 LEGAL PROFESSIONALS											
240 Judges and officers of the Court	NM	3	I	3	I	-	-	-	-	4	I
241 Barristers and advocates	NM	3	I	3	I	-	-	-	-	4	I
242 Solicitors	NM	3	I	3	I	-	-	-	-	4	I
25 BUSINESS AND FINANCIAL PROFESSIONALS											
250 Chartered and certified accountants	NM	3	I	3	I	-	-	-	-	4	I

Table A1 - *continued*

Standard occupational classification unit groups within minor groups	Manual Non-manual	EMPLOYMENT STATUS									
		Self-employed				Managers		Foremen		Apprentices, etc., Employees n.e.c.	
		with employees		without employees							
		S.E.G.	Social Class	S.E.G.	Social Class	S.E.G.	Social Class	S.E.G.	Social Class	S.E.G.	Social Class
251 Management accountants	NM	5.1	II	5.1	II	-	-	-	-	5.1	II
252 Actuaries, economists and statisticians	NM	3	I	3	I	-	-	-	-	4	I
253 Management consultants, business analysts	NM	3	I	3	I	-	-	-	-	4	I
26 ARCHITECTS, TOWN PLANNERS AND SURVEYORS											
260 Architects	NM	3	I	3	I	-	-	-	-	4	I
261 Town planners	NM	-	-	3	I	-	-	-	-	4	I
262 Building, land, mining and 'general practice' surveyors	NM	3	I	3	I	-	-	-	-	4	I
27 LIBRARIANS AND RELATED PROFESSIONALS											
270 Librarians	NM	-	-	-	-	1.2, 2.2	II	-	-	5.1	II
271 Archivists and curators	NM	-	-	-	-	-	-	-	-	5.1	II
29 PROFESSIONAL OCCUPATIONS NEC											
290 Psychologists	NM	3	I	3	I	-	-	-	-	4	I
291 Other social and behavioural scientists	NM	3	I	3	I	-	-	-	-	4	I
292 Clergy	NM	3	I	3	I	-	-	-	-	4	I
293 Social workers, probation officers	NM	-	-	-	-	1.2, 2.2	II	-	-	5.1	II
30 SCIENTIFIC TECHNICIANS											
300 Laboratory technicians	NM	5.1	II	5.1	II	2.2	II	5.1	II	5.1	II
301 Engineering technicians	NM	5.1	II	5.1	II	1.2, 2.2	II	5.1	II	5.1	II
302 Electrical/electronic technicians	NM	5.1	II	5.1	II	1.2, 2.2	II	5.1	II	5.1	II
303 Architectural and town planning technicians	NM	-	-	5.1	II	-	-	-	-	5.1	II
304 Building and civil engineering technicians	NM	-	-	-	-	-	-	-	-	5.1	II
309 Other scientific technicians n.e.c.	NM	5.1	II	5.1	II	1.2, 2.2	II	5.1	II	5.1	II
31 DRAUGHTSPERSONS, QUANTITY AND OTHER SURVEYORS											
310 Draughtspersons	NM	1.1, 2.1	IIIN	12	IIIN	1.2, 2.2	II	5.2	IIIN	6	IIIN
311 Building inspectors	NM	-	-	-	-	-	-	-	-	5.1	II
312 Quantity surveyors	NM	5.1	II	5.1	II	-	-	-	-	5.1	II
313 Marine, insurance and other surveyors	NM	5.1	II	5.1	II	1.2, 2.2	II	5.1	II	5.1	II
32 COMPUTER ANALYST/PROGRAMMERS											
320 Computer analyst/programmers	NM	5.1	II	5.1	II	1.2, 2.2	II	-	-	5.1	II
33 SHIP AND AIRCRAFT OFFICERS, AIR TRAFFIC PLANNERS AND CONTROLLERS											
330 Air traffic planners and controllers	NM	-	-	-	-	-	-	-	-	5.1	II
331 Aircraft flight deck officers	NM	1.1	II	12	II	1.2	II	-	-	5.1	II
332 Ship and hovercraft officers	NM	1.1	II	12	II	1.2	II	-	-	-	-

Table A1 - *continued*

Standard occupational classification unit groups within minor groups	Manual Non-manual	EMPLOYMENT STATUS Self-employed with employees S.E.G.	Social Class	Self-employed without employees S.E.G.	Social Class	Managers S.E.G.	Social Class	Foremen S.E.G.	Social Class	Apprentices, etc., Employees n.e.c. S.E.G.	Social Class
34 HEALTH ASSOCIATE PROFESSIONALS											
340 Nurses	NM	5.1	II	5.1	II	1.2, 2.2	II	5.1	II	5.1	II
341 Midwives	NM	5.1	II	5.1	II	1.2, 2.2	II	5.1	II	5.1	II
342 Medical radiographers	NM	5.1	II	5.1	II	1.2, 2.2	II	5.1	II	5.1	II
343 Physiotherapists	NM	5.1	II	5.1	II	1.2, 2.2	II	5.1	II	5.1	II
344 Chiropodists	NM	5.1	II	5.1	II	1.2, 2.2	II	-	-	5.1	II
345 Dispensing opticians	NM	5.1	II	5.1	II	-	-	-	-	5.1	II
346 Medical technicians, dental auxiliaries	NM	5.1	II	5.1	II	1.2, 2.2	II	5.1	II	5.1	II
347 Occupational and speech therapists, psychotherapists, therapists n.e.c.	NM	5.1	II	5.1	II	1.2, 2.2	II	5.1	II	5.1	II
348 Environmental health officers	NM	-	-	-	-	-	-	-	-	5.1	II
349 Other health associate professionals n.e.c.	NM	5.1	II	5.1	II	-	-	-	-	5.1	II
35 LEGAL ASSOCIATE PROFESSIONALS											
350 Legal service and related occupations	NM	5.1	II	5.1	II	1.2, 2.2	II	-	-	5.1	II
36 BUSINESS AND FINANCIAL ASSOCIATE PROFESSIONALS											
360 Estimators, valuers	NM	5.1	II	5.1	II	1.2, 2.2	II	-	-	5.1	II
361 Underwriters, claims assessors, brokers, investment analysts	NM	1.1, 2.1	II	5.1	II	1.2, 2.2	II	-	-	5.1	II
362 Taxation experts	NM	5.1	II	5.1	II	1.2, 2.2	II	-	-	-	-
363 Personnel and industrial relations officers	NM	5.1	II	5.1	II	-	-	-	-	5.1	II
364 Organisation and methods and work study officers	NM	5.1	II	5.1	II	-	-	-	-	5.1	II
37 SOCIAL WELFARE ASSOCIATE PROFESSIONALS											
370 Matrons, houseparents	NM	1.1, 2.1	II	12	II	1.2, 2.2	II	-	-	7	II
371 Welfare, community and youth workers	NM	-	-	-	-	1.2, 2.2	II	-	-	5.1	II
38 LITERARY, ARTISTIC AND SPORTS PROFESSIONALS											
380 Authors, writers, journalists	NM	1.1, 2.1	II	5.1	II	1.2, 2.2	II	-	-	5.1	II
381 Artists, commercial artists, graphic designers	NM	1.1, 2.1	II	5.1	II	1.2, 2.2	II	5.1	II	5.1	II
382 Industrial designers	NM	1.1, 2.1	II	5.1	II	1.2, 2.2	II	-	-	5.1	II
383 Clothing designers	NM	1.1, 2.1	II	5.1	II	1.2, 2.2	II	-	-	5.1	II
384 Actors, entertainers, stage managers, producers and directors	NM	1.1, 2.1	II	5.1	II	1.2, 2.2	II	-	-	5.1	II
385 Musicians	NM	1.1, 2.1	II	5.1	II	1.2, 2.2	II	-	-	5.1	II
386 Photographers, camera, sound and video equipment operators	NM	1.1, 2.1	IIIN	12	IIIN	1.2, 2.2	II	5.2	IIIN	6	IIIN
387 Professional athletes, sports officials	NM	1.1, 2.1	IIIN	12	IIIN	1.2, 2.2	II	-	-	6	IIIN

43

Standard occupational classification unit groups within minor groups	Manual Non-manual	EMPLOYMENT STATUS									
		Self-employed				Managers		Foremen		Apprentices, etc., Employees n.e.c.	
		with employees		without employees							
		S.E.G.	Social Class	S.E.G.	Social Class	S.E.G.	Social Class	S.E.G.	Social Class	S.E.G.	Social Class
39 ASSOCIATE PROFESSIONAL AND TECHNICAL OCCUPATIONS NEC											
390 Information officers	NM	-	-	-	-	1.2, 2.2	II	-	-	5.1	II
391 Vocational and industrial trainers	NM	5.1	II	5.1	II	1.2, 2.2	II	-	-	5.1	II
392 Careers advisers and vocational guidance specialists	NM	5.1	II	5.1	II	1.2, 2.2	II	-	-	5.1	II
393 Driving instructors (excluding HGV)	NM	2.1	IIIN	12	IIIN	2.2	II	-	-	6	IIIN
394 Inspectors of factories, utilities and trading standards	NM	-	-	-	-	-	-	-	-	5.1	II
395 Other statutory and similar inspectors n.e.c.	NM	-	-	-	-	-	-	-	-	5.1	II
396 Occupational hygienists and safety officers (health and safety)	NM	-	-	-	-	1.2, 2.2	II	-	-	5.1	II
399 Other associate professional and technical occupations n.e.c.	NM	5.1	II	5.1	II	1.2, 2.2	II	5.1	II	5.1	II
40 ADMINISTRATIVE/CLERICAL OFFICERS AND ASSISTANTS IN CIVIL SERVICE AND LOCAL GOVERNMENT											
400 Civil Service administrative officers and assistants	NM	-	-	-	-	-	-	-	-	6	IIIN
401 Local government clerical officers and assistants	NM	-	-	-	-	-	-	5.2	IIIN	6	IIIN
41 NUMERICAL CLERKS AND CASHIERS											
410 Accounts and wages clerks, book-keepers, other financial clerks	NM	1.1, 2.1	IIIN	12	IIIN	-	-	5.2	IIIN	6	IIIN
411 Counter clerks and cashiers	NM	1.1, 2.1	IIIN	12	IIIN	-	-	5.2	IIIN	6	IIIN
412 Debt, rent and other cash collectors	NM	1.1, 2.1	IIIN	12	IIIN	-	-	5.2	IIIN	6	IIIN
42 FILING AND RECORDS CLERKS											
420 Filing, computer and other records clerks (inc. legal conveyancing)	NM	1.1, 2.1	IIIN	12	IIIN	-	-	5.2	IIIN	6	IIIN
421 Library assistants/clerks	NM	-	-	-	-	-	-	5.2	IIIN	6	IIIN
43 CLERKS (NOT OTHERWISE SPECIFIED)											
430 Clerks (n.o.s.)	NM	1.1, 2.1	IIIN	12	IIIN	-	-	5.2	IIIN	6	IIIN
44 STORES AND DESPATCH CLERKS, STOREKEEPERS											
440 Stores, despatch and production control clerks	NM	-	-	-	-	-	-	5.2	IIIN	6	IIIN
441 Storekeepers and warehousemen/women	M	1.1, 2.1	IV	12	IV	2.2	IIIM	8	IIIM	10	IV
45 SECRETARIES, PERSONAL ASSISTANTS, TYPISTS, WORD PROCESSOR OPERATORS											
450 Medical secretaries	NM	1.1, 2.1	IIIN	12	IIIN	-	-	-	-	6	IIIN

Table A1 - *continued*

Standard occupational classification unit groups within minor groups	Manual Non-manual	Self-employed with employees S.E.G.	Self-employed with employees Social Class	Self-employed without employees S.E.G.	Self-employed without employees Social Class	Managers S.E.G.	Managers Social Class	Foremen S.E.G.	Foremen Social Class	Apprentices, etc., Employees n.e.c. S.E.G.	Apprentices, etc., Employees n.e.c. Social Class
451 Legal secretaries	NM	1.1, 2.1	IIIN	12	IIIN	-	-	-	-	6	IIIN
452 Typists and word processor operators	NM	1.1, 2.1	IIIN	12	IIIN	-	-	5.2	IIIN	6	IIIN
459 Other secretaries, personal assistants, typists, word processor operators n.e.c.	NM	1.1, 2.1	IIIN	12	IIIN	-	-	5.2	IIIN	6	IIIN
46 RECEPTIONISTS, TELEPHONISTS AND RELATED OCCUPATIONS											
460 Receptionists	NM	-	-	-	-	-	-	-	-	6	IIIN
461 Receptionist/telephonists	NM	-	-	-	-	-	-	-	-	6	IIIN
462 Telephone operators	NM	-	-	-	-	-	-	5.2	IIIN	6	IV
463 Radio and telegraph operators, other office communication system operators	NM	-	-	-	-	-	-	5.2	IIIN	6	IIIN
49 CLERICAL AND SECRETARIAL OCCUPATIONS NEC											
490 Computer operators, data processing operators, other office machine operators	NM	1.1, 2.1	IIIN	12	IIIN	-	-	5.2	IIIN	6	IIIN
491 Tracers, drawing office assistants	NM	-	-	12	IIIN	-	-	5.2	IIIN	6	IIIN
50 CONSTRUCTION TRADES											
500 Bricklayers, masons	M	1.1, 2.1	IIIM	12	IIIM	2.2	II	8	IIIM	9	IIIM
501 Roofers, slaters, tilers, sheeters, cladders	M	1.1, 2.1	IV	12	IV	2.2	IIIM	8	IIIM	10	IV
502 Plasterers	M	1.1, 2.1	IIIM	12	IIIM	2.2	II	8	IIIM	9	IIIM
503 Glaziers	M	1.1, 2.1	IV	12	IV	2.2	IIIM	8	IIIM	10	IV
504 Builders, building contractors	M	1.1, 2.1	IIIM	12	IIIM	2.2	II	-	-	9	IIIM
505 Scaffolders, stagers, steeplejacks, riggers	M	1.1, 2.1	IV	12	IV	2.2	IIIM	8	IIIM	10	IV
506 Floorers, floor coverers, carpet fitters and planners, floor and wall tilers	M	1.1, 2.1	IIIM	12	IIIM	2.2	II	8	IIIM	9	IIIM
507 Painters and decorators	M	1.1, 2.1	IIIM	12	IIIM	2.2	II	8	IIIM	9	IIIM
509 Other construction trades n.e.c.	M	1.1, 2.1	IV	12	IV	2.2	IIIM	8	IIIM	10	IV
51 METAL MACHINING, FITTING AND INSTRUMENT MAKING TRADES											
510 Centre, capstan, turret and other lathe setters and setter-operators	M	1.1, 2.1	IIIM	12	IIIM	-	-	8	IIIM	9	IIIM
511 Boring and drilling machine setters and setter-operators	M	1.1, 2.1	IV	12	IV	-	-	8	IIIM	10	IV
512 Grinding machine setters and setter-operators	M	1.1, 2.1	IV	12	IV	-	-	8	IIIM	10	IV
513 Milling machine setters and setter-operators	M	1.1, 2.1	IV	12	IV	-	-	8	IIIM	10	IV
514 Press setters and setter-operators	M	1.1, 2.1	IIIM	12	IIIM	-	-	8	IIIM	9	IIIM
515 Tool makers, tool fitters and markers-out	M	1.1, 2.1	IIIM	12	IIIM	2.2	II	8	IIIM	9	IIIM
516 Metal working production and maintenance fitters	M	1.1, 2.1	IIIM	12	IIIM	2.2	II	8	IIIM	9	IIIM
517 Precision instrument makers and repairers	M	1.1, 2.1	IIIM	12	IIIM	2.2	II	8	IIIM	9	IIIM
518 Goldsmiths, silversmiths, precious stone workers	M	1.1, 2.1	IIIM	12	IIIM	2.2	II	8	IIIM	9	IIIM

Standard occupational classification unit groups within minor groups	Manual Non-manual	Self-employed with employees S.E.G.	Self-employed with employees Social Class	Self-employed without employees S.E.G.	Self-employed without employees Social Class	Managers S.E.G.	Managers Social Class	Foremen S.E.G.	Foremen Social Class	Apprentices, etc., Employees n.e.c. S.E.G.	Apprentices, etc., Employees n.e.c. Social Class
519 Other machine tool setters and setter-operators n.e.c. (including CNC setter-operators)	M	1.1, 2.1	IIIM	12	IIIM	-	-	8	IIIM	9	IIIM
52 ELECTRICAL/ELECTRONIC TRADES											
520 Production fitters (electrical/electronic)	M	1.1, 2.1	IIIM	12	IIIM	2.2	II	8	IIIM	9	IIIM
521 Electricians, electrical maintenance fitters	M	1.1, 2.1	IIIM	12	IIIM	2.2	II	8	IIIM	9	IIIM
522 Electrical engineers (not professional)	M	1.1, 2.1	IIIM	12	IIIM	2.2	II	-	-	9	IIIM
523 Telephone fitters	M	-	-	12	IIIM	-	-	8	IIIM	9	IIIM
524 Cable jointers, lines repairers	M	-	-	12	IIIM	-	-	8	IIIM	9	IIIM
525 Radio, TV and video engineers	M	1.1, 2.1	IIIM	12	IIIM	2.2	II	8	IIIM	9	IIIM
526 Computer engineers, installation and maintenance	M	1.1, 2.1	IIIM	12	IIIM	2.2	II	8	IIIM	9	IIIM
529 Other electrical/electronic trades n.e.c.	M	1.1, 2.1	IIIM	12	IIIM	2.2	II	8	IIIM	9	IIIM
53 METAL FORMING, WELDING AND RELATED TRADES											
530 Smiths and forge workers	M	1.1, 2.1	IIIM	12	IIIM	2.2	II	8	IIIM	9	IIIM
531 Moulders, core makers, die casters	M	1.1, 2.1	IIIM	12	IIIM	-	-	8	IIIM	9	IIIM
532 Plumbers, heating and ventilating engineers and related trades	M	1.1, 2.1	IIIM	12	IIIM	2.2	II	8	IIIM	9	IIIM
533 Sheet metal workers	M	1.1, 2.1	IIIM	12	IIIM	2.2	II	8	IIIM	9	IIIM
534 Metal plate workers, shipwrights, riveters	M	1.1, 2.1	IIIM	12	IIIM	2.2	II	8	IIIM	9	IIIM
535 Steel erectors	M	1.1, 2.1	IIIM	12	IIIM	2.2	II	8	IIIM	9	IIIM
536 Barbenders, steel fixers	M	1.1, 2.1	IIIM	12	IIIM	2.2	II	8	IIIM	9	IIIM
537 Welding trades	M	1.1, 2.1	IIIM	12	IIIM	2.2	II	8	IIIM	9	IIIM
54 VEHICLE TRADES											
540 Motor mechanics, auto engineers (inc. road patrol engineers)	M	1.1, 2.1	IIIM	12	IIIM	2.2	II	8	IIIM	9	IIIM
541 Coach and vehicle body builders	M	1.1, 2.1	IIIM	12	IIIM	2.2	II	8	IIIM	9	IIIM
542 Vehicle body repairers, panel beaters	M	1.1, 2.1	IIIM	12	IIIM	2.2	II	8	IIIM	9	IIIM
543 Auto electricians	M	1.1, 2.1	IIIM	12	IIIM	2.2	II	8	IIIM	9	IIIM
544 Tyre and exhaust fitters	M	1.1, 2.1	IV	12	IV	2.2	IIIM	8	IIIM	10	IV
55 TEXTILES, GARMENTS AND RELATED TRADES											
550 Weavers	M	1.1, 2.1	IIIM	12	IIIM	2.2	II	8	IIIM	9	IIIM
551 Knitters	M	1.1, 2.1	IIIM	12	IIIM	2.2	II	8	IIIM	9	IIIM
552 Warp preparers, bleachers, dyers and finishers	M	1.1, 2.1	IIIM	12	IIIM	2.2	II	8	IIIM	9	IIIM
553 Sewing machinists, menders, darners and embroiderers	M	1.1, 2.1	IV	12	IV	-	-	8	IIIM	10	IV
554 Coach trimmers, upholsterers and mattress makers	M	1.1, 2.1	IIIM	12	IIIM	2.2	II	8	IIIM	9	IIIM

Standard occupational classification unit groups within minor groups	Manual Non-manual	EMPLOYMENT STATUS									
		Self-employed				Managers		Foremen		Apprentices, etc., Employees n.e.c.	
		with employees		without employees							
		S.E.G.	Social Class	S.E.G.	Social Class	S.E.G.	Social Class	S.E.G.	Social Class	S.E.G.	Social Class
555 Shoe repairers, leather cutters and sewers, footwear lasters, makers and finishers, other leather making and repairing	M	1.1, 2.1	IIIM	12	IIIM	2.2	II	8	IIIM	9	IIIM
556 Tailors and dressmakers	M	1.1, 2.1	IIIM	12	IIIM	2.2	II	8	IIIM	9	IIIM
557 Clothing cutters, milliners, furriers	M	1.1, 2.1	IIIM	12	IIIM	2.2	II	8	IIIM	9	IIIM
559 Other textiles, garments and related trades n.e.c.	M	1.1, 2.1	IIIM	12	IIIM	2.2	II	8	IIIM	9	IIIM
56 PRINTING AND RELATED TRADES											
560 Originators, compositors and print preparers	M	1.1, 2.1	IIIM	12	IIIM	2.2	II	8	IIIM	9	IIIM
561 Printers	M	1.1, 2.1	IIIM	12	IIIM	2.2	II	8	IIIM	9	IIIM
562 Bookbinders and print finishers	M	1.1, 2.1	IIIM	12	IIIM	2.2	II	8	IIIM	9	IIIM
563 Screen printers	M	1.1, 2.1	IIIM	12	IIIM	2.2	II	8	IIIM	9	IIIM
569 Other printing and related trades n.e.c.	M	1.1, 2.1	IIIM	12	IIIM	2.2	II	8	IIIM	9	IIIM
57 WOODWORKING TRADES											
570 Carpenters and joiners	M	1.1, 2.1	IIIM	12	IIIM	2.2	II	8	IIIM	9	IIIM
571 Cabinet makers	M	1.1, 2.1	IIIM	12	IIIM	2.2	II	8	IIIM	9	IIIM
572 Case and box makers	M	1.1, 2.1	IIIM	12	IIIM	2.2	II	8	IIIM	9	IIIM
573 Pattern makers (moulds)	M	1.1, 2.1	IIIM	12	IIIM	2.2	II	8	IIIM	9	IIIM
579 Other woodworking trades n.e.c.	M	1.1, 2.1	IIIM	12	IIIM	2.2	II	8	IIIM	9	IIIM
58 FOOD PREPARATION TRADES											
580 Bakers, flour confectioners	M	1.1, 2.1	IIIM	12	IIIM	2.2	II	8	IIIM	9	IIIM
581 Butchers, meat cutters	M	-	-	-	-	-	-	8	IIIM	9	IIIM
582 Fishmongers, poultry dressers	M	-	-	-	-	-	-	8	IIIM	9	IIIM
59 OTHER CRAFT AND RELATED OCCUPATIONS NEC											
590 Glass product and ceramics makers	M	1.1, 2.1	IIIM	12	IIIM	2.2	II	8	IIIM	9	IIIM
591 Glass product and ceramics finishers and decorators	M	1.1, 2.1	IIIM	12	IIIM	2.2	II	8	IIIM	9	IIIM
592 Dental technicians	M	1.1, 2.1	IIIM	12	IIIM	2.2	II	8	IIIM	9	IIIM
593 Musical instrument makers, piano tuners	M	1.1, 2.1	IIIM	12	IIIM	2.2	II	8	IIIM	9	IIIM
594 Gardeners, groundsmen/groundswomen	M	1.1, 2.1	IV	12	IV	1.2, 2.2	IIIM	8	IIIM	10	IV
595 Horticultural trades	M	15	IV	15	IV	-	-	15	IIIM	15	IV
596 Coach painters, other spray painters	M	1.1, 2.1	IV	12	IV	2.2	IIIM	8	IIIM	10	IV
597 Face trained coalmining workers, shotfirers and deputies	M	1.1, 2.1	IIIM	12	IIIM	-	-	8	IIIM	9	IIIM
598 Office machinery mechanics	M	1.1, 2.1	IIIM	12	IIIM	2.2	II	8	IIIM	9	IIIM
599 Other craft and related occupations n.e.c.	M	1.1, 2.1	IV	12	IV	2.2	IIIM	8	IIIM	10	IV

Table A1 - *continued*

Standard occupational classification unit groups within minor groups	Manual Non-manual	EMPLOYMENT STATUS									
		Self-employed with employees		Self-employed without employees		Managers		Foremen		Apprentices, etc., Employees n.e.c.	
		S.E.G.	Social Class	S.E.G.	Social Class	S.E.G.	Social Class	S.E.G.	Social Class	S.E.G.	Social Class
60 NCOs AND OTHER RANKS, ARMED FORCES											
600 NCOs and other ranks, UK armed forces	-	-	-	-	-	-	-	-	-	16	-
601 NCOs and other ranks, foreign and Commonwealth armed forces	-	-	-	-	-	-	-	-	-	16	-
61 SECURITY AND PROTECTIVE SERVICE OCCUPATIONS											
610 Police officers (sergeant and below)	NM	-	-	-	-	-	-	5.2	IIIN	6	IIIN
611 Fire service officers (leading fire officer and below)	NM	-	-	-	-	-	-	5.2	IIIN	6	IIIN
612 Prison service officers (below principal officer)	NM	-	-	-	-	-	-	5.2	IIIN	6	IV
613 Customs and excise officers, immigration officers (customs: below chief preventive officer; excise: below surveyor)	NM	-	-	-	-	-	-	-	-	5.1	II
614 Traffic wardens	M/NM	-	-	-	-	-	-	5.2	IIIN	10	IV
615 Security guards and related occupations	M/NM	1.1, 2.1	IV	12	IV	-	-	5.2	IIIN	10	IV
619 Other security and protective service occupations n.e.c.	M/NM	1.1, 2.1	IV	12	IV	-	-	5.2	IIIN	10	IV
62 CATERING OCCUPATIONS											
620 Chefs, cooks	M	1.1, 2.1	IIIM	12	IIIM	1.2, 2.2	II	7	IIIM	7	IIIM
621 Waiters, waitresses	M	-	-	12	IV	-	-	7	IIIM	7	IV
622 Bar staff	M	-	-	12	IV	-	-	7	IIIM	7	IV
63 TRAVEL ATTENDANTS AND RELATED OCCUPATIONS											
630 Travel and flight attendants	M	-	-	12	IIIM	-	-	7	IIIM	7	IIIM
631 Railway station staff	M	-	-	-	-	-	-	8	IIIM	11	V
64 HEALTH AND RELATED OCCUPATIONS											
640 Assistant nurses, nursing auxiliaries	NM	5.1	II	5.1	II	1.2, 2.2	II	5.1	II	5.1	II
641 Hospital ward assistants	M	-	-	-	-	-	-	8	IIIM	10	IV
642 Ambulance staff	M	-	-	-	-	-	-	8	IIIM	9	IIIM
643 Dental nurses	NM	5.1	II	5.1	II	1.2, 2.2	II	5.1	II	5.1	II
644 Care assistants and attendants	M	-	-	-	-	-	-	8	IIIM	10	IV
65 CHILDCARE AND RELATED OCCUPATIONS											
650 Nursery nurses	M	1.1, 2.1	IIIM	12	IIIM	-	-	-	-	7	IIIM
651 Playgroup leaders	NM	2.1	IIIN	12	IIIN	-	-	-	-	6	IIIN
652 Educational assistants	M	-	-	-	-	-	-	-	-	7	IV

48

Table A1 - *continued*

Standard occupational classification unit groups within minor groups	Manual Non-manual	EMPLOYMENT STATUS									
		Self-employed with employees		Self-employed without employees		Managers		Foremen		Apprentices, etc., Employees n.e.c.	
		S.E.G.	Social Class	S.E.G.	Social Class	S.E.G.	Social Class	S.E.G.	Social Class	S.E.G.	Social Class
659 Other childcare and related occupations n.e.c.	M	-	-	12	IV	-	-	7	IIIM	7	IV
66 HAIRDRESSERS, BEAUTICIANS AND RELATED OCCUPATIONS											
660 Hairdressers, barbers	M	-	-	-	-	-	-	7	IIIM	7	IIIM
661 Beauticians and related occupations	M	1.1, 2.1	IV	12	IV	1.2, 2.2	IIIM	8	IIIM	10	IV
67 DOMESTIC STAFF AND RELATED OCCUPATIONS											
670 Domestic housekeepers and related occupations	M	-	-	-	-	-	-	7	IIIM	7	IIIM
671 Housekeepers (non-domestic)	M	-	-	-	-	-	-	7	IIIM	-	-
672 Caretakers	M	-	-	-	-	-	-	8	IIIM	10	IV
673 Launderers, dry cleaners, pressers	M	2.1	IV	12	IV	1.2, 2.2	IIIM	8	IIIM	10	IV
69 PERSONAL AND PROTECTIVE SERVICE OCCUPATIONS NEC											
690 Undertakers	M	1.1, 2.1	IIIM	12	IIIM	1.2, 2.2	II	-	-	-	-
691 Bookmakers	M	1.1, 2.1	IIIM	12	IIIM	1.2, 2.2	II	-	-	-	-
699 Other personal and protective service occupations n.e.c.	M	1.1, 2.1	IV	12	IV	1.2, 2.2	IIIM	8	IIIM	10	IV
70 BUYERS, BROKERS AND RELATED AGENTS											
700 Buyers (retail trade)	NM	-	-	-	-	1.2, 2.2	II	-	-	5.1	II
701 Buyers and purchasing officers (not retail)	NM	-	-	-	-	-	-	-	-	5.1	II
702 Importers and exporters	NM	1.1, 2.1	II	12	II	1.2, 2.2	II	-	-	-	-
703 Air, commodity and ship brokers	NM	1.1, 2.1	II	12	II	1.2, 2.2	II	-	-	-	-
71 SALES REPRESENTATIVES											
710 Technical and wholesale sales representatives	NM	1.1, 2.1	IIIN	12	IIIN	1.2, 2.2	II	-	-	6	IIIN
719 Other sales representatives n.e.c.	NM	1.1, 2.1	IIIN	12	IIIN	1.2, 2.2	II	-	-	6	IIIN
72 SALES ASSISTANTS AND CHECK-OUT OPERATORS											
720 Sales assistants	NM	-	-	-	-	-	-	5.2	IIIN	6	IIIN
721 Retail cash desk and check-out operators	NM	-	-	-	-	-	-	5.2	IIIN	6	IIIN
722 Petrol pump forecourt attendants	NM	-	-	-	-	-	-	5.2	IIIN	6	IIIN
73 MOBILE, MARKET AND DOOR-TO-DOOR SALESPERSONS AND AGENTS											
730 Collector salespersons and credit agents	NM	1.1, 2.1	IV	12	IV	2.2	IIIN	-	-	6	IV
731 Roundsmen/women and van salespersons	M/NM	1.1, 2.1	IIIM	12	IIIM	1.2, 2.2	II	5.2	IIIN	9	IIIM
732 Market and street traders and assistants	NM	1.1, 2.1	IV	12	IV	2.2	IIIN	-	-	6	IV
733 Scrap dealers, scrap metal merchants	NM	1.1, 2.1	IIIN	12	IIIN	1.2, 2.2	IIIN	-	-	-	-

Table A1 - *continued*

Standard occupational classification unit groups within minor groups	Manual Non-manual	EMPLOYMENT STATUS									
		Self-employed				Managers		Foremen		Apprentices, etc., Employees n.e.c.	
		with employees		without employees							
		S.E.G.	Social Class	S.E.G.	Social Class	S.E.G.	Social Class	S.E.G.	Social Class	S.E.G.	Social Class
79 SALES OCCUPATIONS NEC											
790 Merchandisers	NM	-	-	12	IIIN	-	-	-	-	6	IIIN
791 Window dressers, floral arrangers	NM	1.1, 2.1	IIIN	12	IIIN	1.2, 2.2	II	-	-	6	IIIN
792 Telephone salespersons	NM	-	-	12	IIIN	-	-	5.2	IIIN	6	IIIN
80 FOOD, DRINK AND TOBACCO PROCESS OPERATIVES											
800 Bakery and confectionery process operatives	M	1.1, 2.1	IIIM	12	IIIM	-	-	8	IIIM	9	IIIM
801 Brewery and vinery process operatives	M	1.1, 2.1	IIIM	12	IIIM	2.2	II	8	IIIM	9	IIIM
802 Tobacco process operatives	M	-	-	-	-	-	-	8	IIIM	10	IV
809 Other food, drink and tobacco process operatives n.e.c.	M	1.1, 2.1	IV	12	IV	2.2	IIIM	8	IIIM	10	IV
81 TEXTILES AND TANNERY PROCESS OPERATIVES											
810 Tannery production operatives	M	1.1, 2.1	IIIM	12	IIIM	2.2	II	8	IIIM	9	IIIM
811 Preparatory fibre processors	M	1.1, 2.1	IV	12	IV	2.2	IIIM	8	IIIM	10	IV
812 Spinners, doublers, twisters	M	1.1, 2.1	IV	12	IV	2.2	IIIM	8	IIIM	10	IV
813 Winders, reelers	M	1.1, 2.1	IV	12	IV	2.2	IIIM	8	IIIM	10	IV
814 Other textiles processing operatives	M	1.1, 2.1	IV	12	IV	-	-	8	IIIM	10	IV
82 CHEMICALS, PAPER, PLASTICS AND RELATED PROCESS OPERATIVES											
820 Chemical, gas and petroleum process plant operatives	M	1.1, 2.1	IV	12	IV	2.2	IIIM	8	IIIM	10	IV
821 Paper, wood and related process plant operatives	M	1.1, 2.1	IIIM	12	IIIM	-	-	8	IIIM	9	IIIM
822 Cutting and slitting machine operatives (paper products etc.)	M	1.1, 2.1	IIIM	12	IIIM	2.2	II	8	IIIM	9	IIIM
823 Glass and ceramics furnace operatives, kilnsetters	M	-	-	-	-	-	-	8	IIIM	9	IIIM
824 Rubber process operatives, moulding machine operatives, tyre builders	M	1.1, 2.1	IIIM	12	IIIM	-	-	8	IIIM	9	IIIM
825 Plastics process operatives, moulders and extruders	M	1.1, 2.1	IV	12	IV	2.2	IIIM	8	IIIM	10	IV
826 Synthetic fibre makers	M	-	-	-	-	-	-	8	IIIM	10	IV
829 Other chemicals, paper, plastics and related process operatives n.e.c.	M	1.1, 2.1	IV	12	IV	-	-	8	IIIM	10	IV
83 METAL MAKING AND TREATING PROCESS OPERATIVES											
830 Furnace operatives (metal)	M	1.1, 2.1	IIIM	12	IIIM	-	-	8	IIIM	9	IIIM
831 Metal drawers	M	1.1, 2.1	IIIM	12	IIIM	-	-	8	IIIM	9	IIIM
832 Rollers	M	1.1, 2.1	IIIM	12	IIIM	2.2	II	8	IIIM	9	IIIM
833 Annealers, hardeners, temperers (metal)	M	1.1, 2.1	IV	12	IV	-	-	8	IIIM	10	IIIM

Table A1 - *continued*

Standard occupational classification unit groups within minor groups	Manual Non-manual	EMPLOYMENT STATUS									
		Self-employed				Managers		Foremen		Apprentices, etc., Employees n.e.c.	
		with employees		without employees							
		S.E.G.	Social Class	S.E.G.	Social Class	S.E.G.	Social Class	S.E.G.	Social Class	S.E.G.	Social Class
834 Electroplaters, galvanisers, colour coaters	M	1.1, 2.1	IIIM	12	IIIM	-	-	8	IIIM	9	IIIM
839 Other metal making and treating process operatives n.e.c.	M	1.1, 2.1	IIIM	12	IIIM	-	-	8	IIIM	9	IIIM
84 METAL WORKING PROCESS OPERATIVES											
840 Machine tool operatives (inc. CNC machine tool operatives)	M	1.1, 2.1	IV	12	IV	-	-	8	IIIM	10	IV
841 Press stamping and automatic machine operatives	M	1.1, 2.1	IV	12	IV	2.2	IIIM	8	IIIM	10	IV
842 Metal polishers	M	1.1, 2.1	IIIM	12	IIIM	2.2	II	8	IIIM	9	IIIM
843 Metal dressing operatives	M	1.1, 2.1	IV	12	IV	-	-	8	IIIM	10	IV
844 Shot blasters	M	-	-	12	IV	-	-	8	IIIM	10	IV
85 ASSEMBLERS/LINEWORKERS											
850 Assemblers/lineworkers (electrical/electronic goods)	M	1.1, 2.1	IV	12	IV	-	-	8	IIIM	10	IV
851 Assemblers/lineworkers (vehicles and other metal goods)	M	-	-	12	IV	-	-	8	IIIM	10	IV
859 Other assemblers/lineworkers n.e.c.	M	-	-	12	IV	-	-	8	IIIM	10	IV
86 OTHER ROUTINE PROCESS OPERATIVES											
860 Inspectors, viewers and testers (metal and electrical goods)	M	-	-	12	IV	-	-	8	IIIM	10	IV
861 Inspectors, viewers, testers and examiners (other manufactured goods)	M	-	-	-	-	-	-	8	IIIM	9	IIIM
862 Packers, bottlers, canners, fillers	M	1.1, 2.1	IV	12	IV	-	-	8	IIIM	10	IV
863 Weighers, graders, sorters	M	-	-	-	-	-	-	8	IIIM	10	IV
864 Routine laboratory testers	M	-	-	-	-	-	-	8	IIIM	9	IIIM
869 Other routine process operatives n.e.c.	M	1.1, 2.1	IV	12	IV	2.2	IIIM	8	IIIM	10	IV
87 ROAD TRANSPORT OPERATIVES											
870 Bus inspectors	M	-	-	-	-	-	-	8	IIIM	-	-
871 Road transport depot inspectors and related occupations	M	-	-	-	-	-	-	8	IIIM	-	-
872 Drivers of road goods vehicles	M	1.1, 2.1	IIIM	12	IIIM	2.2	II	8	IIIM	9	IIIM
873 Bus and coach drivers	M	1.1, 2.1	IIIM	12	IIIM	2.2	II	-	-	9	IIIM
874 Taxi, cab drivers and chauffeurs	M	1.1, 2.1	IIIM	12	IIIM	2.2	II	-	-	9	IIIM
875 Bus conductors	M	-	-	12	IV	-	-	-	-	10	IV
88 OTHER TRANSPORT AND MACHINERY OPERATIVES											
880 Seafarers (merchant navy); barge, lighter and boat operatives	M	1.1, 2.1	IV	12	IV	-	-	8	IIIM	10	IV
881 Rail transport inspectors, supervisors and guards	M	-	-	-	-	-	-	8	IIIM	9	IIIM
882 Rail engine drivers and assistants	M	-	-	-	-	-	-	-	-	9	IIIM

Standard occupational classification unit groups within minor groups	Manual Non-manual	EMPLOYMENT STATUS									
		Self-employed				Managers		Foremen		Apprentices, etc., Employees n.e.c.	
		with employees		without employees							
		S.E.G.	Social Class	S.E.G.	Social Class	S.E.G.	Social Class	S.E.G.	Social Class	S.E.G.	Social Class
883 Rail signal operatives and crossing keepers	M	-	-	-	-	-	-	8	IIIM	9	IIIM
884 Shunters and points operatives	M	-	-	-	-	-	-	8	IIIM	9	IIIM
885 Mechanical plant drivers and operatives (earth moving and civil engineering)	M	1.1, 2.1	IIIM	12	IIIM	2.2	II	8	IIIM	9	IIIM
886 Crane drivers	M	-	-	-	-	-	-	8	IIIM	9	IIIM
887 Fork lift and mechanical truck drivers	M	-	-	12	IIIM	-	-	8	IIIM	9	IIIM
889 Other transport and machinery operatives n.e.c.	M	1.1, 2.1	IIIM	12	IIIM	-	-	8	IIIM	9	IIIM
89 PLANT AND MACHINE OPERATIVES NEC											
890 Washers, screeners and crushers in mines and quarries	M	-	-	-	-	-	-	8	IIIM	10	IV
891 Printing machine minders and assistants	M	1.1, 2.1	IIIM	12	IIIM	-	-	8	IIIM	9	IIIM
892 Water and sewerage plant attendants	M	-	-	-	-	-	-	8	IIIM	11	V
893 Electrical, energy, boiler and related plant operatives and attendants	M	-	-	-	-	-	-	8	IIIM	10	IV
894 Oilers, greasers, lubricators	M	-	-	-	-	-	-	8	IIIM	9	IIIM
895 Mains and service pipe layers, pipe jointers	M	1.1, 2.1	IV	12	IV	-	-	8	IIIM	10	IV
896 Construction and related operatives	M	1.1, 2.1	IV	12	IV	2.2	IIIM	8	IIIM	10	IV
897 Woodworking machine operatives	M	1.1, 2.1	IIIM	12	IIIM	2.2	II	8	IIIM	9	IIIM
898 Mine (excluding coal) and quarry workers	M	1.1, 2.1	IV	12	IV	2.2	IIIM	8	IIIM	10	IV
899 Other plant and machine operatives n.e.c.	M	1.1, 2.1	IV	12	IV	2.2	IIIM	8	IIIM	10	IV
90 OTHER OCCUPATIONS IN AGRICULTURE, FORESTRY AND FISHING											
900 Farm workers	M	15	IV	15	IV	-	-	15	IIIM	15	IV
901 Agricultural machinery drivers and operatives	M	15	IV	15	IV	-	-	15	IIIM	15	IV
902 All other occupations in farming and related	M	15	IV	15	IV	-	-	15	IIIM	15	IV
903 Fishing and related workers	M	2.1	IV	12	IV	2.2	IIIM	8	IIIM	10	IV
904 Forestry workers	M	15	IV	15	IV	-	-	15	IIIM	15	IV
91 OTHER OCCUPATIONS IN MINING AND MANUFACTURING											
910 Coal mine labourers	M	-	-	-	-	-	-	8	IIIM	10	IV
911 Labourers in foundries	M	-	-	-	-	-	-	8	IIIM	11	V
912 Labourers in engineering and allied trades	M	-	-	-	-	-	-	8	IIIM	11	V
913 Mates to metal/electrical and related fitters	M	-	-	-	-	-	-	-	-	10	IV
919 Other labourers in making and processing industries n.e.c.	M	-	-	-	-	-	-	8	IIIM	11	V

Table A1 - *continued*

Standard occupational classification unit groups within minor groups	Manual Non-manual	Self-employed with employees S.E.G.	Social Class	Self-employed without employees S.E.G.	Social Class	Managers S.E.G.	Social Class	Foremen S.E.G.	Social Class	Apprentices, etc., Employees n.e.c. S.E.G.	Social Class
92 OTHER OCCUPATIONS IN CONSTRUCTION											
920 Mates to woodworking trades workers	M	-	-	-	-	-	-	-	-	9	IIIM
921 Mates to building trades workers	M	2.1	IV	12	IV	-	-	8	IIIM	10	IV
922 Rail construction and maintenance workers	M	-	-	-	-	-	-	8	IIIM	10	IV
923 Road construction and maintenance workers	M	2.1	V	12	V	-	-	8	IIIM	11	V
924 Paviors, kerb layers	M	1.1, 2.1	IV	12	IV	-	-	8	IIIM	10	IV
929 Other building and civil engineering labourers n.e.c.	M	1.1, 2.1	V	12	V	-	-	8	IIIM	11	V
93 OTHER OCCUPATIONS IN TRANSPORT											
930 Stevedores, dockers	M	1.1, 2.1	V	12	V	-	-	8	IIIM	11	V
931 Goods porters	M	1.1, 2.1	V	12	V	2.2	IIIM	8	IIIM	11	V
932 Slingers	M	-	-	-	-	-	-	8	IIIM	9	IIIM
933 Refuse and salvage collectors	M	-	-	-	-	-	-	8	IIIM	11	V
934 Driver's mates	M	-	-	-	-	-	-	-	-	11	V
94 OTHER OCCUPATIONS IN COMMUNICATION											
940 Postal workers, mail sorters	M	-	-	-	-	-	-	8	IIIM	10	IV
941 Messengers, couriers	M	-	-	12	V	-	-	8	IIIM	11	V
95 OTHER OCCUPATIONS IN SALES AND SERVICES											
950 Hospital porters	M	-	-	-	-	-	-	8	IIIM	10	IV
951 Hotel porters	M	-	-	-	-	-	-	8	IIIM	10	IV
952 Kitchen porters, hands	M	-	-	-	-	-	-	8	IIIM	11	V
953 Counterhands, catering assistants	M	-	-	-	-	-	-	7	IIIM	7	IV
954 Shelf fillers	NM	-	-	-	-	-	-	-	-	6	IV
955 Lift and car park attendants	M	-	-	-	-	-	-	8	IIIM	11	V
956 Window cleaners	M	1.1, 2.1	V	12	V	2.2	IIIM	8	IIIM	11	V
957 Road sweepers	M	-	-	-	-	-	-	8	IIIM	11	V
958 Cleaners, domestics	M	1.1, 2.1	V	12	V	2.2	IIIM	8	IIIM	11	V
959 Other occupations in sales and services n.e.c.	M	1.1, 2.1	IV	12	IV	1.2, 2.2	IIIM	8	IIIM	10	IV
99 OTHER OCCUPATIONS NEC											
990 All other labourers and related workers	M	2.1	V	12	V	-	-	8	IIIM	11	V
999 All others in miscellaneous occupations n.e.c.	M	1.1, 2.1	IIIM	12	IIIM	-	-	8	IIIM	9	IIIM
- Inadequately described occupations	-	17	-	17	-	17	-	17	-	17	-
Occupations not stated	-	-	-	-	-	-	-	-	-	17	-

Appendix B. The role of the OPCS Occupational Information Unit

The Occupational Information Unit has been set up within OPCS to support users of SOC. It provides a central point for advice and information on coding occupations and has responsibility for updating and revising SOC. Staff of the Unit log comments and queries arising from census coding and other major SOC applications in OPCS, the Employment Group of Departments, and elsewhere. The Unit keeps in touch with developments in occupational classification, including computer assisted methods and changes in occupational terminology.

The address of the Occupational Information Unit is:

OPCS
Segensworth Road
Titchfield
Fareham
Hants PO15 5RR

Telephone Titchfield (0329) 42511 Extension 3639/3503

Appendix C. List of terms and abbreviations

Institutions

OPCS   *Office of Population Censuses and Surveys.* Government department responsible for carrying out censuses of population, registration of births, marriages and deaths, a range of sample surveys, and other functions involving classification of occupations. Sponsored with ED and participated in the development of SOC and has responsibility under an Interdepartmental Management Board for maintaining SOC (see also Appendix B).

ED   *Employment Group of Departments.* Responsible for implementing government employment, training, and manpower policies and for producing a range of statistics concerning the labour force and its attributes, including occupation. Sponsored the development of CODOT and now SOC, and with OPCS is one of the two main government users of SOC.

IER   *Institute for Employment Research, University of Warwick.* Collaborated with OPCS and ED to develop SOC. Also involved in developing a version of the International Standard Classification of Occupations (ISCO) suitable for use in the European Community.

ILO   *International Labour Office.* Based in Geneva. Responsible for developing and maintaining the International Standard Classification of Occupations (ISCO).

Occupational classifications and classificatory terms

CO80   *OPCS Classification of Occupations 1980.* This was used in classifying occupational information obtained via the 1980 Census of Population and has been used in many survey and other applications during the nineteen eighties. Its predecessor was the Classification of Occupations 1970; its successor is the Standard Occupational Classification (SOC).

OCG   *Operational Coding Group.* One of the 350 most detailed categories into which job titles and activities were coded in the 1981 Census, using the Classification of Occupations 1980 (CO80). The detailed occupational classification used in analysing census data was an elaboration of this.

CODOT   *Classification of Occupations and Directory of Occupational Titles.* This is the classification used in many Employment Department and other applications until replaced by the Standard Occupational Classification. It was designed to provide a high level of detail suitable for distinguishing skill specialisms and for use in job placement etc.

KOS   *Key Occupations for Statistics.* This is a classification obtained by aggregating the categories of CODOT to provide a detailed occupational breakdown suitable for statistical work. It has been used in coding occupational information from large sample sources such as the New Earnings Survey.

Condensed KOS   This was created by further aggregation of the KOS categories. It could be matched by aggregation of categories distinguished in CO80 and thus provided a 'bridge' between the two approaches to occupational classification represented by CODOT and CO80. It has been widely used in presenting occupational statistics.

55

SOC   *Standard Occupational Classification.*

OUG   *Occupational Unit Group. One of the 371* most detailed categories into which job titles and activities are coded using SOC.*

Minor Group   *One of 77 categories into which the 371 Occupational Unit Groups can be aggregated in SOC.*

Sub-major Group   *One of 22 categories into which the 371 Occupational Unit Groups can be aggregated in SOC.*

Major Group   *One of 9 categories into which the 77 Minor Group Groups can be aggregated in SOC.*

ISCO 88   *International Standard Classification of Occupations 1988. Classification of Occupations developed by the International Labour Office (ILO). Revised in 1988. Similar structure and level of detail to SOC, but with some important differences of detail.*

Socio-economic classifications

SC   *Social Class based on Occupation (formerly Registrar General's Social Class). Scale for classifying persons into one of six groups. Developed and maintained by OPCS and its predecessor and widely used in censuses, surveys, and other research. Derived by grouping occupational categories and making further discriminations by reference to the job-holder's status in employment (self-employed, supervisor, etc.). Now based on SOC.*

SEG   *Socio-economic Groups. Classification of persons into one of 17 groups taking account of occupation, status in employment, and size of employing establishment. Widely used in censuses and surveys. Now based on SOC.*

Major official sources of occupational data

Census   *National Census of Population. Carried out every ten years throughout UK (last in 1981, next in 1991). Collects social and economic information about all members of the population, but occupation and other items are coded and analysed for a 10% sample only.*

LFS   *Labour Force Survey. Large annual household survey carried out in Great Britain by OPCS on behalf of the Employment Department since 1973. Collects information about many attributes of household members, particularly those related to labour force participation (e.g. occupation).*

NES   *New Earnings Survey. Large annual survey carried out by the Employment Department. It is based on a sample of employees identified through their National Insurance numbers and collects information about them, including occupation and earnings, from their employers.*

---

*   Section 3.3 in SOC Volume 1 incorrectly quoted 374 unit groups.

Printed in the UK for HMSO
Dd 294055 C55 4/91 Ed(288736)